Third Culture Faithful

Third Culture Faithful

Empowered Ministry for Multi-Ethnic Believers and Congregations

Mario Manuel Catalino Melendez

An Alban Institute Book
ROWMAN & LITTLEFIELD
Lanham • Boulder • New York • London

Published by Rowman & Littlefield
An imprint of The Rowman & Littlefield Publishing Group, Inc.
4501 Forbes Boulevard, Suite 200, Lanham, Maryland 20706
www.rowman.com

6 Tinworth Street, London SE11 5AL, United Kingdom

Copyright © 2020 by The Rowman & Littlefield Publishing Group, Inc.

All rights reserved. No part of this book may be reproduced in any form or by any electronic or mechanical means, including information storage and retrieval systems, without written permission from the publisher, except by a reviewer who may quote passages in a review.

British Library Cataloguing in Publication Information Available

Library of Congress Cataloging-in-Publication Data Is Available

Library of Congress Control Number: 2020946783

ISBN 978-1-5381-4725-2 (cloth)
ISBN 978-1-5381-4726-9 (pbk)
ISBN 978-1-5381-4727-6 (electronic)

To my departed friend and professor Dr. Ken Easley. You used biblical theology to help me learn who I am and my place in the Missio Dei. May this book help others find their unique place, as you helped me.

1 Tim. 1:17 τῷ δὲ βασιλεῖ τῶν αἰώνων, ἀφθάρτῳ, ἀοράτῳ, μόνῳ θεῷ, τιμὴ καὶ δόξα εἰς τοὺς αἰῶνας τῶν αἰώνων · ἀμήν.

To my dear friends and acquaintances who are in a mixed marriage. May this work be a place for you to better understand your children, and may this work help you help them understand their glorious place in the Gospel story!

Contents

Introduction		1
1	The Psychology of Third Culture Syndrome	13
2	Your Parishioner, the Third Culture Kid	29
3	Your Ministry for the Third Culture Kid	53
4	Your Pastor, the Third Culture Kid	95
Conclusion: Points of Application		125
Notes		129
Bibliography		135
Index		143
About the Author		145

Introduction

In 1960 Martin Luther King Jr. told his interviewer on Meet the Press, "it is appalling that the most segregated hour of Christian America is eleven o'clock on Sunday morning."[1] Sadly in the twenty-first century the quote remains true. Baylor University found in 2012 that only 12 percent of US congregations qualify as multi-ethnic (a congregation where no one ethnicity exceeds 80%).[2]

> More congregations seem to be growing more attentive to the changing demographics outside their doors, and as U.S. society continues to diversify by race and ethnicity, congregations' ability to adapt to those changes will grow in importance. (Michael O. Emerson, PhD, provost of North Park University in Chicago)[3]

In my personal denomination, Southern Baptist, I estimate that less than 3 percent are multi-ethnic of some 50,000 churches. In light of this truth, where should people of mixed ethnicities attend church?

The Pew Research Center found in 1967 that 3 percent of marriages were interracial, but as of 2015 14 percent of all marriages in the United States are interracial. Further research shows 30 percent of all minority marriages are now interracial.[4] Not only has diversity in marriage grown but also the number of those who identify with two or more ethnicities.

- US Census Bureau found that, in 2013, about 9 million Americans chose two or more racial categories when asked about their race. The Census Bureau first started allowing people to choose more than one racial category to describe themselves in 2000. Between 2000 and 2010, the number of white and black biracial Americans was more than double, while the

population of adults with a white and Asian background increased by 87 percent.[5]
- The Census Bureau projects that the multiracial population will be 20 percent by 2050.[6]
- The Pew Research survey finds that biracial adults with a white and American Indian background comprise half of the country's multiracial population—by far not only the country's largest multiracial group but also the one whose members are the least likely to consider themselves "multiracial" despite their mixed-race background.[7]

This mixed group can be called "biracial" or what will be utilized in this work "Third Culture Kids."[8] A TCK does not fully reflect their parents' respective cultures nor the culture they live in. I propose that believers of mixed backgrounds need not live outside the divided church, but rather be trained and empowered because they are uniquely qualified to help unite the church. "By not fitting neatly into one category, however, researchers say the growing number of multiracial Americans may help the rest of the population develop the flexibility to see people as more than just a demographic—and to move away from race as a central marker of identity."[9]

The following are the famous multi-ethnic personalities

1) Ann Curry: Japanese/Caucasian
2) Barack Obama: Kenyan/Caucasian
3) Bruno Mars: Puerto Rican/Ashkenazi Jewish/Filipino/Spanish
4) Derek Jeter: African American/Caucasian
5) Dwayne Johnson: Samoan/African Canadian/Caucasian
6) Kamala Harris: Indian/Jamaican
7) Kimora Lee Simmons: African American/Japanese
8) Keanu Reeves: Chinese-Hawaiian/Caucasian
9) Maya Rudolph: African American/Ashkenazi Jewish
10) Meghan Markle: African American/Caucasian
11) Naomi Campbell: Chinese/Jamaican
12) Naomi Osaka: Japanese/Haitian
13) Norah Jones: Indian/Caucasian
14) Ryan Lochte: Cuban/Caucasian
15) Thandie Newton: Zimbabwean/Caucasian
16) Soledad O'Brien: Cuban/Caucasian
17) Tiger Woods: Thai/Chinese/Caucasian/African American/Native American
18) Tracee Ellis Ross: Ashkenazi Jewish/African American
19) Trevor Noah: Xhosa/Caucasian

My name is Dr. Mario Manuel Catalino Melendez. I am Filipino, Cajun French, Spaniard, English, plus I grew up around the deaf community and I married a Scottish-Irish girl! Within my family we have a spectrum of skin color and at least five practiced languages (Tagalog, Cajun French, Spanish, Sign Language, and English). What this means is that I don't know if I want Filipino, Cajun, or good ole Americana food. Though some family members are Roman Catholic, Pentecostal, or Baptist, we all seem to have the same heart struggle of not feeling like we truly belong wherever we attend. Whatever congregation we attend, we are always the "only" of some kind there. Sadly, as a result of this feeling, subsequent generations are less faithful to a local church congregation. I have learned over time that my family is not the only one to suffer in this way.

My life has been a conglomeration of cross-cultural experiences. I was first raised in an independent fundamental Baptist church and then in a Southern Baptist Convention (SBC). I attended a Baptist elementary and then a Pentecostal high school. After high school, I attended Samford University, Leavell College, Union University, Mid-America Baptist Theological Seminary, and finally completed my PhD at New Orleans Baptist Theological seminary in biblical interpretation. I have served in nine ministerial positions at English, Spanish, and Asian churches. If all this diversity has taught me anything, I have learned that the church is still segregated and I rarely fit. I have experienced prejudice of some church members, and care from other members who understand the unifying power of the gospel. My story parallels with many of my cousins' and friends', who qualify as Third Culture, thus I believe I can speak to the topic at hand.

So where does a mixed kid find a sense of belonging? I was raised in a family that proudly watched and rewatched every Star Trek show and movie. For myself, my brother, and many cousins, Star Trek offered an on-screen utopia where not only were mixed marriages permissible (Star Trek had the first interracial on-screen kiss), but mixed beings were an asset to the Enterprise, Voyager, and Deep Space 9 (*Discovery doesn't exist in my mind*). In this utopia I found great respect and admiration of the mixed minority. Any time a captain had a pressing mission, there always was a mixed person necessary to the resolution. The often-understated role of Deanna Troi (a half human/half Betazoid empath) helped me to believe that talents and gifts handed down through our families can help many races. Through Star Trek I learned that like the mixed crew members, I too must learn to reflect and fit in for the greater good, but not to the detriment of my respective cultures and their gifts I possess. Sadly, we have not developed a proper warp drive nor built the Enterprise and begun the Federation of planets. So, for most of my life, I found my place in my local karate school. I began training in karate at the age of nine, and later trained in judo, and jujitsu. The commonality between these schools was their diversity yet unity in the art form. I guess you could say that martial arts were my Federation of planets, for my church was not!

When I moved to Memphis to earn my first master's degree from Union University, I met two crucial people, Dr. Kendell Easley and Bryan Loritts. Though I only got close to Ken, both men spoke prophetically and as a result helped me to rest in my identity. They shared two crucial aspects, which will be explained in greater depth later in this work. First, I am like Timothy, who was half Greek and half Jewish, and as a result I have a unique capability. Bryan in his work, *Right Color Wrong Culture*, explains that mixed people (what fits into his label as C2) are not only welcomed into the church, but like Star Trek's mixed officers, they are necessary for unifying the church! Loritts stated,

> C2 leadership [TCK] is essential at the highest echelons of any organization if they want to be multiethnic. A C2 is a person who is culturally flexible and adaptable without becoming ethnically ambiguous or hostile. . . . A C2 has a wide range of relationships and can navigate various ethnicities and cultures while maintaining his unique identity all at once. C2s are typically classified by high levels of cultural intelligence and sensitivity. They not only are committed to nudging the organization forward in matters of ethnicity, but they also know the rate in which they need to push without alienating their constituency.[10]

Second, as Ken taught me, I need to focus on being part of the church. Ken wrote a wonderful work *Illustrated Guide to Biblical History*, which was a supplemental reading for our Biblical Survey courses at Union University. I recall the first time I heard Ken give his one sentence summary of scripture; "The Lord God is graciously building a kingdom of redeemed people for their joy and his glory." That night in class, I finally understood my joy shouldn't be held in how well I fit into the local parish, but in the glorious eternal kingdom that Christ has welcomed me into.

The aim of this work is to introduce the concept of third culture syndrome, explain common realities of this syndrome in multi-ethnic parishioners, suggest ministry to them, and to advocate for empowering third cultured ministers. Though the recent outcry for minority leadership in churches and academies has been ignored, the development of third cultured believers may yield persons capable of answering the cry, for third cultured leaders can uniquely aid both sides in the unifying process of the body of Christ.[11]

THE PROPOSITION OF UNITY

Before delving into ministering and empowering multi-ethnic people, one should ask why we should strive for ethnic unity in the church? I am often told by parishioners that we are separate for stylistic reasons. By contrast, in certain circles, forming multi-ethnic churches seems to be the "current cool" thing to do. However, there should be a biblical foundation for all ecclesiological endeavors. So, is the church mandated to become multi-ethnic? If a church does not diversify, are they disobedient? If multi-ethnicity is a biblical thrust, why is it not espoused or taught at most pastoral training schools or from most pulpits?

Some churches that desire to diversify have the desire but lack the resources to effectively pursue multi-ethnicity. Reality is that your church may be in an area with virtually no ethnic diversity. Other churches that have a diverse community and desire are led by wrong motivations.

> The most common motivation that I have heard is Guilt. This is especially true for many white churches. The argument goes: "Whites have marginalized and oppressed blacks for so long, churches need to make it right by 'reaching out' to different races and ethnicities." While guilt has its place, this emotion will hardly give churches the determination they need to persevere through the difficulties of becoming multi-ethnic.
>
> Another common motivation is fear. Christians fear lots of things about being in a mono-ethnic church. We fear that as neighborhood demographics change we will lose people. We fear that we will become irrelevant in the community. We fear being racist, or classist, or elitist. Fear, too, has its place. But that won't keep churches moving toward a multi-ethnic vision.[12]

If a church were to set aside political reasons, such as the mentioned guilt reason, and current cool trends, one should recognize three major biblical reasons to have ethnic unity in the church.

Reason 1: It Is a Picture of the Gospel

In being a picture of the gospel, the TCK can better appreciate their mixed background.

I advocate for multi-ethnic churches because it reflects the true nature of the gospel and the nature of God. A diverse church is a picture of the true nature of the gospel, for the gospel is God reconciling sinful humanity to himself through the work of Jesus (Rom. 5:10, Col. 1:20), so "that we should be called sons and daughters of God" (1 John 3:1). Sin at the Tower of Babel led to division and confusion (Gen. 11:1–9). But, when Pentecost happened in Acts 2, Babel's sin problem was defeated, and division became unity (Acts 2:42). Likewise, in a multi-ethnic church there is reconciliation between peoples that the world prefers to keep separate. In the United States we have a saying, "birds of a feather flock together," but in the gospel we are "one in Christ."

In other words, it's not about racial reconciliation; it's about reconciling men and women to God through faith in Jesus Christ, and about reconciling a local church to the principles and practices of New Testament congregations of faith, such as existed at Antioch and Ephesus.[13]

As a picture of the Trinity a multi-ethnic church contains distinct people focused on one purpose. The Trinity, in the most elementary of terms, is a picture of three distinct persons unified as one. If the church is to be the "body" of Christ (His representative) then what a better way to represent God than distinct peoples being unified as one? In John 17:20–23 Jesus prays a prayer asking the Father to help his disciples, and those after them, to be unified.

> [20]I do not ask for these only, but also for those who will believe in me through their word, [21]that they may all be one, just as you, Father, are in me, and I in you, that they also may be in us, so that the world may believe that you have sent me. [22]The glory that you have given me I have given to them, that they may be one even as we are one, [23]I in them and you in me, that they may become perfectly one, so that the world may know that you sent me and loved them even as you loved me.

Let's face it, no church will be perfect, but we can get a sense and joy out of striving to be more like Him than we were yesterday. Thus, Mark Deymaz rightly asserted, "I believe that local churches are biblically mandated to respond in some way to the prayer of Christ in John 17:20–23."[14] The diversifying/unifying of the church is a beautiful privilege given the opportunity and means.

If opportunity to diversify a church were to exist, there are a handful of stances the church can take in answering the ministerial opportunity. When analyzing churches that I have been involved in I have found Darrin Patrick's spectrum of churches to be useful:

Church in the City—Have an inward look and not on what the city is, and does. The goal is to get people in to hear the gospel. Little outreach, much in reach.

Church against the city—The city is irredeemable, and a disgrace. Therefore we'll stay here and do it the way we've always done it. Little outreach, little truth being taught.

Church of the City—Takes all that the city holds and teaches and adopts it for their own, and to their detriment.—so relevant they forget the Gospel.

Church for the city—one that holds tightly to the Gospel, but confronts the pressing needs of their surrounding neighborhoods. A model of engagement where a church speaks the truth of the gospel and is not afraid to uphold a biblical worldview and moral standard. Such a church proclaims the truths of Scripture with passion, clarity, and boldness. At the same time, though, this is a church that commits itself to seeking the shalom, the flourishing, of the city.[15]

A church for the city is one that is in a diverse area and constantly strives "to become all things to all men to reach some." We should note this missional calling applies to all churches regardless of ethnicity. The end of a gospel picture through multi-ethnicity is the gospel contextualized to many. When diversity exists in the congregation, the gospel can cross many social barriers. Sadly, the diverse congregation implication of the gospel is rarely taught at pastoral training institutions; I will make proposals to amend this void in chapter 4.

Reason 2: It Is a Picture of Heaven on Earth

In being a picture of heaven on earth, the TCK can find a place in the local church.

If you're like me, you grew up in a church that corporately quotes and memorizes scripture. A frequently quoted verse in our service is the Lord's model prayer. In this prayer there is a section that we often don't consider in church ecclesiology. "Thy kingdom come thy will be done here on earth as it is in heaven" (Matt. 6:10). Growing up in a Baptist church, I heard this passage preached dozens of times, but never heard the ethnic implication till my friend and professor Dr. Matt Akers read this verse in light of Revelation 7 (all the following quotes come from his published podcast—*Salmerica*).[16]

> [9]After this I looked, and behold, a great multitude that no one could number, from every nation, from all tribes and peoples and languages, standing before the throne and before the Lamb, clothed in white robes, with palm branches in their hands, [10]and crying out with a loud voice, "Salvation belongs to our God who sits on the throne, and to the Lamb!" [11]And all the angels were standing around the throne and around the elders and the four living creatures, and they fell on their faces before the throne and worshiped God, [12]saying, "Amen! Blessing and glory and wisdom and thanksgiving and honor and power and might be to our God forever and ever! Amen."

Matt observed in this passage that two groups of people begin the chapter, and yet are considered one people at the end. Matt calls this "unidiversity," for every language and people is seen by John, yet unified together. If we were to read Revelation 7 passage and apply it "here on earth as it is in heaven," we would find four applicable points. (1) "We are one in Christ despite our heritage." The beautiful thing about the gospel is that we have more in common with fellow Christians than we do with our relatives who are not believers! When the church at Ephesus was suffering with divisions, Paul reminds them of the gospel and their commonalities.

> Ephesians 4:1 I therefore, a prisoner for the Lord, urge you to walk in a manner worthy of the calling to which you have been called, ²with all humility and gentleness, with patience, bearing with one another in love, ³eager to maintain the unity of the Spirit in the bond of peace. ⁴There is one body and one Spirit—just as you were called to the one hope that belongs to your call— ⁵one Lord, one faith, one baptism, ⁶one God and Father of all, who is over all and through all and in all.

(2) "Oneness in Christ should be a present reality." If indeed heaven is a unified people worshipping together, then that should be our aim here on earth. (3) "True unity does not equate to colorblindness." I love that when John looks into heaven he does not declare, "I don't see color." In this passage, there is appreciation of culture and language in the body of Christ. Thus, we should strive to worship together, even if it is linguistically messy. (4) "True unity does pursue harmony." In John's vision the unity of heaven is only accomplished via Christ and results in them harmoniously praising God together. I am often asked if I support/espouse "racial reconciliation." I always respond that I support biblical reconciliation, for without Christ man-made reconciliation will always break down at some point. *Furthermore, the term "racial-reconciliation" is now a political term, which I avoid using any politicalized terms.*

So, if we pray "your kingdom come your will be done here on earth as it is in heaven," what is the multi-ethnic church? Possibly a simple answer is that a multi-ethnic church is a glimpse of heaven on earth. I love how Sandra Richter defines heaven on earth, "It is the People of God, in the Place of God, dwelling in the Presence of God."[17] If indeed the presence of the Lord is where two or more are gathered, we should strive to make that gathering look like heaven!

Reason 3: It Strengthens the Church

In strengthening the Church, the TCK becomes a uniquely gifted and uniquely valued member.

Maybe up to this point you are struggling to see the concept of diversity as a "biblical mandate." So, let me offer a rational missional reason by reflecting on Paul's teaching in 1 Corinthians 12. Paul began the chapter by essentially stating all people have been given a useful spiritual gift. In verses 12–13 Paul continues this teaching on being useful for the body of Christ,

> 12 For just as the body is one and has many members, and all the members of the body, though many, are one body, so it is with Christ. 13 For in one Spirit we were all baptized into one body—Jews or Greeks, slaves or free—and all were made to drink of one Spirit.

Some have taken this passage to only refer to the Catholic Church (universal church). That may be a portion of the scriptural understanding. However, I believe Paul is telling the Corinthian church to quit being divisive and realize that all believers are needed and useful for the edification of their church.

This teaching is very different from our American church landscape. As a friend once observed we can basically understand separate congregations by their spiritual gift. Teachers in one congregation, preachers in another, musicians in another, another has the servants, another has leaders, and so on for the full twenty-two gifts listed in the New Testament. So, what would it look like if churches in America were to be diverse because of gifting? I would like to believe churches that are stagnate or declining would be growing, and Islam would not be the world's fastest growing religion.

If we are indeed in a holy war (Eph. 6:12) then we need every capable believer to work out their spiritual gifts for the sake of the church (Rom. 12). Returning back to the bridge of the enterprise, one finds a very diverse group of officers gifted and trained in special fields. While indeed Commander Worf can take the captain's chair if need be, the unique giftedness of Captain Piccard better serves the enterprise. Likewise, the captain could command the tactical station, but a Klingon warrior mind often proves most useful at that station. Unity in the body of Christ should not equate to uniformity, but rather as Matt terms it "unidiversity." I believe for the sake of the church; the mixed person is critical to helping the various parties better understand each other. Scripture holds at least one historical example of how a mixed believer can be crucial, for he helped during the Temple construction (1 Kings 7:13—Hyram of Tyre and Naphtalie). The following chart shows the numerous mixed people within scripture.

Other notable mixed peoples in scripture are as follows:

Ishmael (Genesis 16)
Keturah's sons (Genesis 25)
Esau's children: Er, Onan, Shelah, Perez, Zerah (Genesis 36)
Ephraim and Manasseh (Genesis 48)
Gershom and Eliezer (Exodus 18)
Caleb (Numbers 32)
Shelomith's son (Leviticus 24)
Rahab's children (Matt. 1:5)
Ruth's children (Ruth 4)
Huram-Abi (2 Chron. 2:13)

Solomon (2 Samuel 12)
Absalom (2 Samuel 13)
Ahab's children (2 Kings 10)
Children of the exile (Ezra 10)
Samaritans (2 Kings 17; Ezra 4:2–11)
Timothy (Acts 16)
Jesus (Matthew 1)

Reason 4: The Gospel to the Third Generation

In caring for the third generation, the TCK will grow up appreciating the church.

As will be discussed later, I truly believe that entire generations have been lost because a church was solely focused upon the generation at hand (the mono-ethnic generation). This short sightedness led churches to having ethnic missions that split, latter only to die off thus leaving the second and third generations to be unchurched and have no relation to the still going mother church. In Acts 2:38–39 Peter answers to those who asked how to be saved, and throws in this interesting addition, "For the promise is for you and for your children and for all who are far off, everyone whom the Lord our God calls to himself." As an Evangelical Baptist I do not believe that your child is a part of the redeemed just because you are. However, I do believe that the promise/provision of salvation is available to your children and every subsequent generation should they "repent and believe in the Lord Jesus Christ for the forgiveness of sins." With the growing populace of multi-ethnic marriages, and multi-ethnic children, a gospel concern for the children gives reason for a multi-ethnic ministry. I hope this book will help shed light on the unique needs and qualifications of these mixed generations. Unless churches are purposefully ministering to these generations, there will be even more churches closing their doors in the coming years, as this populace grows.

QUESTIONS FOR CONVERSATIONS

TCK:

- What is your mixed story?
- How have you felt growing up or visiting various churches?
- What place did/do you run to for belonging?

Minister/Parent and TCK:

- Read Genesis 11, Acts 2, and Revelation 7: In what ways does the gospel corrects the sin problem of Babel.
- Were you ever taught that unity of ethnicities was an implication of the gospel?
- When was the first time you recognized the church segregation?
- What exactly about the segregation bothers you (if anything at all)?
- Why do you believe the division still persists?
- Of the four propositions of unity, which is the most compelling reason and which is the least compelling reason to you?
- What key insight did you glean from this section? And how do you plan to integrate the insight into your life/ministry?

SUGGESTED READING

Building a Healthy Multi-Ethnic Church: Mandate, Commitments and Practices of a Diverse Congregation by Mark DeYmaz.
Intensional: Kingdom Ethnicity in a Divided World by D. A. Horton.
"Multiracial in America: Proud, Diverse and Growing in Numbers" by Kim Parker, Juliana Horowitz, Rich Morin, and Mark Lopez.
"The Joyful Pursuit of Multi-Ethnic Churches" by Jemar Tisby.

Chapter 1

The Psychology of Third Culture Syndrome

I remember hundreds, if not thousands, of days when I was asked by someone, "What are you?"

> The categorization of multiracial individuals is often difficult because of the ambiguity in their racial appearance. Precisely because of this ambiguity, multiracial individuals are frequently bombarded with the question, "What are you?" often coupled with responses such as, "Really? You don't look it," or "Are you sure?"[1]

Explaining my heritage and linguistic capability is like trying to teach a northerner how to make Gumbo. I can explain the basic premise of the recipe, but in truth, my family doesn't cook with recipes, we just know what is needed and when. Likewise, I had no clue how to fully explain myself until I came to the knowledge of third culture syndrome. Before this syndrome was formalized, most people of mixed background were forced to pick one or a couple definers. Picking a singular definer is often detrimental to the person, and often yields the question of "what is wrong with me?"[2] While I am ¾ European by blood, I look like a tall Asian or Hispanic, pending my clothing and glasses. Yet, a former student in Memphis had the same amount of Filipino heritage yet looked like a Viking. He and I conversed quite often about Filipino food, culture, and of course Arnel Pineda, of the band journey. Yet we had no clue how to explain how we felt and looked to the world. Peter's notation in 1 Pet. 2:10 has become especially close to me in my process of learning my identity and place, "You once were not a people, but now you are a people of God." In a sense, prior to third culture syndrome being formalized, mixed people did not have a matrix by which to understand themselves, thus many have fallen prey to whims and ways of a single culture. The danger of this historical handling of mixed people is the ignoring of unique qualifications of the mixed individual.

HISTORY OF THIRD CULTURE SYNDROME CHART

In the 1950s John and Ruth Useem, after studying the children of expat Americans, proposed the terms "third culture kid" and "third culture syndrome."[3] The Useems created these terms when they sociologically observed expatriate communities in India (1952–1953). The observed neither fully embraced their new culture, nor fully held onto their "passport home." According to Pollock and Van Reken, the Useems realized that "the expatriates had formed a lifestyle that was different from either their home [parent's culture] or their host culture [current surrounding culture]" thus forming a third or "interstitial culture," a "culture between cultures" lifestyle.[4]

Over the years, other titles have been developed and defended as more definitively accurate descriptions for this type of child including global nomad (McCaig, 1994; Langford, 1988),[5] globally mobile children (Grimshaw & Sears, 2008; Hayden, 2006),[6] cross-cultural kids (Lee, 2008; Pollock & Van Reken, 2009),[7] or transcultural children (Frederick, 1996).[8] The recent work of Pollock and Van Reken has moved TCK studies into more realms than international expats.[9] The majority of TCK research focuses upon how to help TCKs return to their "passport home" (Klemens, 2008; Schulz, 1985; Sotherden, 1992; Thurston-Gonzalez, 2009; Wrobbel, 2005),[10] identity development (Lyttle, Barker, & Cornwell, 2011; Moore, 2011; Schaetti, 2000),[11] and functional abilities as adult TCKs (Fail, 2002).[12] However, after reviewing the literature on TCKs, only one source sheds any light on TCKs attributes within the Christian context (Ulrika Ernvik, 2019).[13] The state of research reveals the need for a work such as this one to help shed light on the TCKs unique abilities within the church.

LET'S TALK TERMS: THIRD CULTURE/ BIRACIAL/MULTI-ETHNIC

One of my wife and my favorite shows is Penn and Teller's *Fool Us*. What is interesting about this show is how the two magicians try to guess the method the performer utilized. Penn once said that the lingo they utilize may sound nonsensical to the audience, but within the explanation are words which an average person can utilize to research and further grow in their magic knowledge. I am a proponent of utilizing a similar methodology when teaching or writing on any subject. I try to utilize as many revealing terms as possible so the reader can go forth and understand more.

When considering the topic at hand, ministering to mixed people, there are a plethora of terms that could be utilized; third culture, biracial, multi-ethnic, and cross-cultural. Each one of these terms is a valid name to ascribe to someone of mixed heritage. However, each term will only yield certain types of data. I have decided to utilize the term "third culture" because the research within that field avails more psychological research and social interaction research. While the term "biracial" has indeed been utilized for researching people of mixed heritage, the term seems to be more concerned with black-white studies than with other minority groups. Biracial studies are useful to aid some, however when someone has more than two ethnic backgrounds, some of the dual nature of biracial studies doesn't speak to the third or even fourth nature. Furthermore, biracial studies do not necessarily equate to cross-cultural studies. Third culture research, however, primarily focuses upon the cultural benefits and cultural struggles.

If the aim is to help the mixed parishioner and unify the divided church, then there needs to be more than just a racial component. There needs to be a better grasp of cultural impacts. For instance, I know a Korean-white man who lives in Alabama, has a southern accent, loves country music, and shrugs his shoulders at the comment "aren't you Korean?" Helping this person grow into their half nature and utilizing both for the sake of the gospel requires a vast number of tools and data.

Due to the cultural component of TCK studies, I will primarily utilize the term "third culture," or TCK throughout this work. I will however at times mention multi-ethnic, mixed kid, or mixed heritage to refer to the same topic. I encourage any reader desiring to continue research to search out works on all the terms and find the middle ground of application for you. Suggested works will come at the end of each chapter, pulling from numerous fields of study. Please keep in mind that the further reading sections contain works that are not all written by Christians, and some of the ministerial works are not orthodox. However, these works can contribute to researching the noted fields.

WHO IS A THIRD CULTURE KID?

I personally define a third culture kid as one who does not fully reflect their parents' respective cultures nor the culture they live in. This definition most closely resembles that of the David Pollock.

> A Third Culture Kid (TCK) is a person who has spent a significant part of his or her developmental years outside the parent's culture. The TCK frequently

builds relationships to all of the cultures, while not having full ownership in any. Although elements from each culture may be assimilated into the TCK's life experience, the sense of belonging is in relationship to others of similar background.[14]

However, recent works of David Pollock and Ruth Reken have expanded the populace that fit within the name third culture kid. The following list is from their third edition.[15]

- A *cross-cultural kid (CCK)* is a person who is living or has lived in—or meaningfully interacted with—two or more cultural environments for a significant period of time during childhood (up to age 18).
- An *adult CCK (ACCK)* is a person who has grown up as a CCK.
- *Traditional TCKs:* Children who move into another culture with parents due to a parent's career choice.
- *Children from bi/multicultural homes:* Children born to parents from at least two cultures. May or may not be of the same race.
- *Children from bi/multiracial homes:* Children born to parents from at least two races. May or may not be of the same culture.
- *Children of immigrants:* Children whose parents have made a permanent move to a new country where they were not originally citizens.
- *Educational CCKs:* Children who may remain in their home or passport country but are sent to a school (e.g., an international school) with a different cultural base and student mix than the traditional home culture or its schools.
- *Children of refugees:* Children whose parents are living outside their original country or place due to circumstances they did not choose, such as war, violence, famine, or natural disasters.
- *Children of borderlanders:* Children who cross borders frequently, even daily, as they go to school, or whose parents work across national borders.
- *Children of minorities:* Children whose parents are from a racial or ethnic group that is not part of the majority race or ethnicity of the country in which they live.
- *International adoptees:* Children adopted by parents from another country other than the one of that child's birth.
- *Domestic TCKs:* Children whose parents have moved in or among various subcultures within that child's home country.

While the amended list is welcomed, for the purpose of this work, the TCK that will be discussed is the multi-ethnic. Most multi-ethnic people fit into several groups in the new amended list of TCKs. For instance, President Barak Obama fits into six categories: biracial, bicultural, TCK, minority, and educational CCK. This interesting makeup confounded the news and other media who had never described someone who did not fit into one nice box on the census. Thus, most media outlets chose to box President Obama into the African American community and culture. (The census was amended during his presidency to permit multiple ethnic selection.) In his book *Dreams from My Father*, President Obama constantly articulates the angst and struggle he dealt with as a TCK.[16] To this day, few have articulated how the mixed nature of President Obama aided him in being the first minority president.[17]

The primary reason for focusing upon multi-ethnic people as the TCK is that American culture typically divides visually, especially when it comes to churches. When someone sees me, they immediately assume I am some sort of minority, for I look the part. Yet when a third culture non-multiethnic person is met, such as a former student who was a missionary kid from Kenya, people automatically assume that he is a "white guy," though he often said "NO I AM KENYAN!" While Zac is indeed a TCK, he would struggle to stand in the gap in helping heal the church divide, for he is not part of an ethnic minority. Many times in the minority communities you will hear, "you aren't one of us," said to the person raised in the culture. Thus, if the aim of this work is to help churches train up people to help heal the divide, possessing various ethnicities is probably the best place to begin. As will be discussed later, sometimes a mixed person needs encouragement to grow in the knowledge and culture of one of their respective ethnicities. So, if a church or entity were purposefully looking to unite their divided context, I propose a mixed person to be the person who helps step in the void.

Questions for Conversations

TCK:

- Which of the populaces listed earlier do you fit within?

    Minister/Parent and TCK:

- Who do you know that is a TCK?
- Can you name some famous TCKs?
- What key insight did you glean from this section? And how do you plan to integrate the insight into your life/ministry?

THIRD CULTURE DIFFERENCE

In my years of ministry, I have worked at or visited numerous churches of varying denominations and ethnicities. In this process, I have observed cultural norms within the mainstream denominational churches. Furthermore, I have observed family units within majority and minority cultures and deduced

Table 1.1 Culture Chart

Majority Culture/Church Culture	Topic	Minority Cultures/Church Culture
Self	Survival Concern	Community
Personal Control	Control of Life	Fate of God
Tasks	Concern at Gatherings	Human Interaction
Immediate	Family	Extended
Younger Generations	Generational Leadership	Elder Generations
Reserved	Emotion	Expressive
Designated/Patriarchal	Gender Roles	Flexible/Matriarchal
Linear/Organized	Communication	Integrated/Responsive
Direct	Conflict Resolution	Indirect

Source: Adapted from Ernvik, *Third Culture Kids*, 136–37.

that much of the church norm is also found within the respective family unit. Though indeed there are outliers in this survey, I think the cultural chart can help delineate the divide (see table 1.1).

While table 1.1 is a general summary, I have found that the table is rarely wrong. If my mono-ethnic friends do not fit into all of the cultural points, they are usually no more than too shy of the whole list. Thus, there is indeed a need for someone to walk the middle to help mitigate cultural conflicts, if unity is to be achieved.

As I have lived my diverse life and built friendships with other diverse people, I have noticed that we all seem to struggle in the same way. Considering

Table 1.2 Benefits and Challenges of Diverse People

Benefit	Challenge
Adaptability	Lack of True Cultural Balance
Blending In	Defining the Difference
Less Prejudice	More Prejudice
Importance of Now	Delusion of Choice
Appreciative of Authority	Mistrustful of Authority
	Perceived Arrogance
Observational Skills	
Social Skills	
Linguistic Skills	
Rootlessness	Restlessness
Large Number of Relationships	
Deep Valued Relationships	
	Early Maturation
	Delayed Adolescence

Source: Adapted from Pollock and Van Renken, *Third Culture Kids*, 139–228.

the abovementioned list, we tend to fluctuate between the two sides. Also, we all seem to have the same strengths and weaknesses. Again, Pollock and Reken have listed and discussed these commonalities. Table 1.2 shows a quick summary of their findings.

These markers can not only highlight who has the psychological third culture syndrome, but also introduce the benefits and challenges of living with third culture syndrome. Most TCKs who I know call themselves a chameleon, for they fluctuate between cultural norms.[18] Likewise, most TCKs who I know deal with almost all of the earlier challenges.

IN WHAT WAYS ARE TCKS DIFFERENT?[19]

They

- Hold world views that can be 180 degrees different from their peers.
- Understand that there are many ways of doing things.
- Are used to having diversity in relationships.
- Relate differently.
- Are worldly wise, mature, well-versed in places, peoples, cultures, and languages.
- Have more in common with internationals than with domestic peers.
- Are hidden immigrants.

Growing up as a TCK will affect who I am:
  I might feel like

- I have hard time answering the question "Where are you from?"
- Its easier to say "hello" than "goodbye."
- It's hard to feel like I belong.
- I am not sure where home is.

If I grew up as a TCK I might

- Be a chameleon-quick to adjust to a new environment.
- Be a good observer.
- Feel rootless and restless.
- Be very independent.
- Often feel different form others.
- Feel like an outsider.

The plus side of being a TCK includes

- Learning new languages.
- Meeting new people.
- Seeing and experiencing many places.
- Having confidence in travel and starting anew.
- Learning to be creative.
- Understanding that there can be more than one way to look at the same thing.
- Being a good storyteller.

I might have developed

- Cross-cultural skills.
- Observation skills.
- Adaptability skills.
- Social skills.

The flipside might include

- Having to say frequent goodbyes.
- Leaving pets and friends behind.
- Having to find new friends.
- Having to wear masks to feel accepted.
- Being all too familiar with pain.
- Not knowing my own country as well as other places I've lived in.
- Being critical of many things, but especially of home-country peers.
- Being perceived as arrogant because of a different world view.

TCKs often continue to move around because we

- Are used to it.
- Want to continue to discover new parts of the world.
- Never feel at home.
- Love the adventure.
- Visit friends around the world.
- Want to escape.

RESPONSE TO TCK DIFFERENCE

Growing up I often heard weird things said to or about me. I have also uttered the same responses about other TCKs not realizing that these sayings are observational responses to third culture syndrome's affect upon the person. I've always been accused of being "an old soul." This "old soul" of mine has been a ministerial God sent in helping minister, especially to senior saints. On the other hand, when compared to my peers, I have been called immature, and in truth feel that I matured later than my buddies. So, which is it? Was I mature or immature for my age? I've been called flexible for I can walk in and out of cultural situations with ease. Yet I've been called rootless and in need of staying put for a while. I've been called very loving and accepting. Yet several of my mono-ethnic minority friends have called me "more prejudice," because I don't replicate their boisterous voices concerning cultural/political issues.

As will be discussed in chapter 2, TCKs are often accused of being one thing when reality is that they are only articulating/behaving from one side of themselves.[20] As a result, many TCKs are often labeled as being a minority, or being labeled as a sellout to the white culture. These accusations are often extremely hard for the TCK to hear and often result in them asking "Who am I? Can I trust? And what's wrong with me?"[21]

These questions and observations highlight the typical TCK as a big picture person and one who fluctuates to be on both sides. As will be discussed later, Timothy is able to be a big picture person and utilizes his life as a means of ministering to both Jews and Greeks. In our US church culture, these responses will tend to push the TCK away from fellowship, for they are merely being who God created them to be, a go-between. It is up to the minister and their parents to help the TCK navigate these tough statements and to accept the unique abilities which lay behind them.

Questions for Conversations

TCK:

- In what way do you relate to the three charts above? I recommend you write or circle the aspects that relate to you, for these will be discussed throughout this work.
- Which aspects best describe your respective parents? (I suggest marking them—so you can see how you compare to them)

Minister/Parent and TCK:

- Which of these aspects do you recognize in your TCK?
- Did reading any of these aspects give you an "aha" moment? If so, which ones and why?
- What key insight did you glean from this section? And how do you plan to integrate the insight into your life/ministry?

THIRD CULTURE COMMON

One might read the term "culture" and ask how people of varying ethnicities and cultures can classify as "a culture?" My simple answer is that we mixed kids just relate, for we all live in the "in-between." Our flexible nature finds commonality and peace with other flexible peoples, more than it does with mono-ethnic/mono-cultural peoples.[22] Within the TCK community, there is a sense of belonging for we don't dread explaining ourselves. When TCKs congregate, there is just a beautiful sense of belonging in the mix.

When I coached judo at Union University, I taught the previously mentioned Kenyan American, a Chinese American, a Brazilian American, a Hungarian American, a Taiwanese American, and a Guatemalan American. I like to think these students came to the judo club because of my mad judo skills, but the reality was that these students were already congregating on campus for they were third culture common. After the preliminary introductions of name and backgrounds, we no longer discussed the diversity, but rather lived in the commonality. We helped each other at times when anxiety rose regarding cultural norms, and we celebrated each other's minority cultural holidays and customs when they felt homesick. What was interesting was how much each person deviated from the cultural norms listed in the last chart. Most of us were half and half, whereas my friends previously mentioned, from only one culture, were almost all of the respective traits.

While each TCK will be unique in how much of the respective traits they possess, their innate ability to fluctuate to the opposite yields a cultural commonality. This flexibility is why TCKs are such an asset to be considered in ministerial roles. While we love to congregate together, our ability to flip from one side to the other gives the Apostle Paul's "all things to all men" a literal reality in the TCK.

THE DIFFERENCE SPECTRUM

In reflecting upon my mixed judo students, I recall a broad spectrum of how they handled their mixed nature. At times a student would not acknowledge their non-American heritage. At times a student would not acknowledge their white American heritage. Some students integrated the two, and others overcompensated toward the one which they perceived the more accepted nature. Returning to my utopian examples, in Star Trek there is a broad spectrum of acceptance, denial, integration, compensation, or deception as to one's personhood. The author of *Among Worlds*, September 2010 republished in Ernvik (113–119) provided a handful of animal illustrations to adequately describe the spectrum of TCKs.

Butterfly Style

Definition: Fully adopts one culture or even overcompensates by becoming strictly one sided.
Advantages: Identifies with one culture easily.
Disadvantages: Conflicts with other culture. Some may perceive them to be a "sellout."
Star Trek Character: Spock (Vulcan/human). Spock, though half human and half Vulcan is constantly reminded that he is half human. Furthermore, Spock's intense Vulcan nature leads many to call him names such as "pointy ears," "green blooded," and "logical robot." The persistent reflection of his Vulcan nature is probably because Spock finds human nature to be "illogical" or possibly even inferior.

Chameleon Style

Definition: Blends in with the surroundings, by reflecting that which they are around.
Advantages: "A person using this style possess the ability to adapt and blend in. He often can be a mediator between the two worlds. He can depend on his own TCK experience to help him, and he can share a broadened worldview with others."[23]
Disadvantages: "A chameleon identity-style will seem inconsistent. Some days one way, other days another way. People may question, 'who is this person—really—at his core?'"[24]
Star Trek Character: Deanna Troi (Betazoid/human). Deanna served as the enterprises' ship counselor. Her ability as an empath allowed her to read people's emotions, but she did not over utilize her telepathic abilities as her tenuous Betazoid mother. Deanna had all the capabilities of both her human father and Betazoid mother. By utilizing both sides capabilities Deanna is able to reflect an acceptable character in any situation. As a chameleon Deanna is able to be a middle person in confrontational encounters.

Tasmanian Devil Style

Definition: This style constantly emphasizes how they are different. "These responses come from the TCK avoiding having his identity suppressed or assimilated by the surrounding culture."[25]
Advantages: Brings outside perspective.
Disadvantages: Confrontational.
Star Trek Character: B'Elanna Torres (human/Klingon). The best Tasmanian devil that I can think of from the Trek is B'Elanna. Torres is half Klingon and human, born to a human father who is racist toward

Klingons. As a child she overheard her father complaining about living with two Klingons (she and her mother). As a result, B'Elanna is self-loathing toward her Klingon side, and constantly identifies as human (though having a Klingon appearance). B'Elanna so much hated her Klingon heritage that she had the doctor remove all Klingon DNA from her unborn child, Voyager (S E). Though B'elanna doesn't flip flop in identity as some Tasmanians do, she does fulfill the reality that she could have been an asset, but instead provides zero aid in Klingon-human relations.

Mule Style

Definition: One who blends two cultures.
Advantage: No severe cultural conflict, so he avoids the extremes, "middle ground culture."
Disadvantages: Can end up avoiding the pronounced strengths unique to each culture. Thus, often perceived as "bland or neutral."
Star Trek Character: Linnis Paris (human/Ocampan). Linnis was the first mixed child of a Delta Quadrant relationship. Aboard the Voyager, Linnis reflected the acceptable strengths of both backgrounds, but did not deviate far enough to one side or another to truly be noted as either race. As a result, Voyager fans often struggle to really articulate Linnis as a character.

Platypus Style

Definition: This TCK possess select characteristics of each culture.
Advantages: They are typically more positive for they choose the positive traits of each culture.
Disadvantages: May seem like a "patchwork-unintegrated, odd, atypical-when compared to anyone else."[26]
Star Trek Character: K'Ehleyr (human/Klingon). In my opinion, she was the only woman who ever seemed a true match for Worf. K'Ehleyr embodies the Platypus quite well. Introduced in the Next Generation, K'Ehleyr worked as an ambassador for the Klingon empire, however did not fully embody Klingongs for she was half human. Unlike others mentioned, K'Ehleyr integrated characteristics of the two cultures into her being. Thus, she was indeed a warrior, but one of human free will (unlike Klingon women). She was authoritative like a Klingon, but compassionate like a human. The list of this antithesis goes on, but the result is that she is a beautiful yet confusing character. I think K'Ehleyr has the greatest impact upon Worf's story throughout TNG and DS9.

Turtle Style

Definition: Cultural introvert. They often believe they can't fit in or will make mistakes, thus they don't try.
Advantages: Prevents heartache, and avoids conflicts and cultural mistakes.
Disadvantages: Feels isolated and lonely.
Star Trek Character: Simon Tarses (human/Romulan). Though only appearing in one episode (TNG S4 E21), Simon Tarses is a sad picture of the typical turtle. Because the federation is categorically prejudice toward Romulans, Simon never admitted to his heritage. Thus, he "lied about his heritage to enter Star Fleet." Simon, however, was not a vile human hating Romulan, but the result of a union between lovers. Due to the Romulan prejudice, Simon never spoke up, nor truly let anyone know him. Simon's fear was of being killed or hated, so he never entered social norms. As a result, Simon acted like the turtle and retreated into himself never revealing his true nature.

I have observed these six types of TCK throughout my encounters, and within my family. The most common styles that I encounter in churches are the butterfly (sellout), chameleon (blend in), and the Tasmanian devil (the different). Personally, I fall into the chameleon style, for I have always reflected cultures in which I am surrounded. As noted by the advantages and disadvantages lists, each of these styles can contribute to the church, but must be tempered or encouraged at the right time. Once again it is worthwhile reiterating what Loritts noted,

> C2 leadership [TCK] is essential at the highest echelons of any organization if they want to be multiethnic. A C2 is a person who is culturally flexible and adaptable without becoming ethnically ambiguous or hostile. . . . A C2 has a wide range of relationships and can navigate various ethnicities and cultures while maintaining his unique identity all at once. C2s are typically classified by high levels of cultural intelligence and sensitivity. They not only are committed to nudging the organization forward in matters of ethnicity, but they also know the rate in which they need to push without alienating their constituency.[27]

As we move further into ministering to and empowering TCKs to heal the divide, it may be worthwhile helping the TCK determine which style best fits them, and possibly determine if their style is best suited for the church at that time. As will be discussed in chapter 4 of this work, the right style at the right time is necessary for helping a multi-ethnic church to form. However, in the end every style has something to contribute!

Questions for Conversations

TCK:

- Of the noted animal styles, which style do you best relate to?
- If you have siblings, which animal do they best relate to?
- Which animal type most frustrates you to be around, and why?

Minister/Parent and TCK:

- Which of these animal types do you most recognize in your TCK(s)?
- If you had a preference, which animal type would you prefer to be around and why?
- What key insight did you glean from this section? And how do you plan to integrate the insight into your life/ministry?

THIRD CULTURE QUESTIONS

As a child of the 1990s I have a strange affection for 1990s Christian pop. Michael W. Smith's "Place in This World" (1990) has often been an anthem I rocked out to. Thankfully, I never had the big hair, but I did have the honest question of trying to find my place in this world. Modern TCK studies had determined that every TCK has to work through a set of common questions. "I have found that there are three questions most TCKs ask themselves again and again. Each question has a strong emotion connected to it."

- Who am I?
- Can I trust?
- What's wrong with me?[28]

According to Ernvik these questions do not have to be answered.[29] While maturing, every human may ask the good question, "Who am I?" Differing from the norm, the TCK will always ask these three questions throughout their life. Though Ernvik says these do not have to be answered, I believe every Christian TCK must answer three similar questions.

- Why don't I feel comfortable at my church?
- Who should I listen to?
- How does the gospel apply to me?

These questions require a lifetime of discipleship to answer and are constantly reasked by the TCK. I believe that by understanding the TCK and developing purposeful ministries these questions will not only be answered but yield candidates to step into the church divide and help bring about healing.

APPLICATION

As noted in the introduction, the multi-ethnic populace of the United States is growing at an extraordinary rate. "The share of multiracial babies has risen from 1% in 1970 to 10% in 2013. As a result, multiracial adults currently make up 6.9% of the adult American population."[30] This chapter can be applied in four ways. (1) To understand this populace, one must read broadly and carefully observe those within this group. The reading load is daunting and honestly quite difficult to assimilate, but the result is extremely rewarding for those who are mixed or minister to the mixed. (2) Observe those of mixed heritage and prayerfully consider where they fit within the spectrum. (3) Realize that the TCK is rarely going to feel fully at home in your church, thus they will often struggle to grasp how the gospel applies to their life. (4) Pray that God will help raise up a TCK to help heal the church divide.

Questions for Conversations
TCK:

- Have you noticed a rise in TCK/multi-ethnic people in media? (We often notice the rise faster than mono-ethnic people.)

Minister/Parent and TCK:

- Ask the TCK to articulate their answer to the six questions, and carefully take notes as to how it makes them feel.
- With the rise of mixed marriages and mixed children, how is your church/ministry preparing to purposefully diversify and reach this populace?
- What are the implications if churches/ministries do not purposefully reach the rising minority and mixed populations?
- What key insight did you glean from this section? And how do you plan to integrate the insight into your life/ministry?

SUGGESTED READING

Equally Yoked: A Premarital Counseling Primer for Multiethnic Christian Couples by Matthew R. Akers.
"The Interpretation of Multiracial Status and Its Relation to Social Engagement and Psychological Well-Being" by Kevin R. Binning, Miguel M. Unzueta, Yuen J. Huo, and Ludwin E. Molina.

"Multiracial Identity Integration: Perceptions of Conflict and Distance among Multiracial Individuals" by Chi-Ying Cheng and Fiona Lee.

"'Mixed' Results: Multiracial Research and Identity Explorations" by Sarah E. Gaither.

What Are You?: Voices of Mixed-Race Young People by Pearl Fuyo Gaskins.

Ministering in Honor-Shame Cultures: Biblical Foundations and Practical Essentials by Jayson Georges and Mark D. Baker.

The 3D Gospel: Ministry in Guilt, Shame, and Fear Cultures by Jayson Georges.

Third Culture Kids: A Gift to Care For by Ulrika Ernvik.

Finding Home: Third Culture Kids in the World by Rachel Jones.

"The Biracial Advantage" by Rachel Jatson.

Right Color, Wrong Culture: The Type of Leader Your Organization Needs to Become Multiethnic by Bryan Loritts.

Honor and Shame: Unlocking the Door by Roland Muller.

The Oxford Handbook of Multicultural Identity by Peter E. Nathan, Verónica Benet-Martínez, and Ying-Yi Hong.

"Multiracial in America: Proud, Diverse and Growing in Numbers" by Kim Parker, Juliana Horowitz, Rich Morin, and Mark Lopez.

Third Culture Kids: Growing Up among Worlds, revised ed. by David C. Pollock and Ruth E. Van Reken.

Challenging Multiracial Identity by Spencer Rainier.

I'm Chocolate, You're Vanilla: Raising Healthy Black and Biracial Children in a Race-Conscious World by Marguerite Wright.

Chapter 2

Your Parishioner, the Third Culture Kid

My first house in urban Memphis got broken into six times. The first culprit was caught by the police. As a result, I was summoned by the district attorney to give a victim testimony. Upon arriving to court, I was greeted by someone in Spanish. So, I changed mindset and began speaking with this nice lady. When the bailiff entered, he asked if the victims of case number X were present. I raised my hand and stated that I was present. The nice Spanish lady looked at me with her eyes wide open and said, "You don't need a translator!" To my astonishment, the lady was a court translator who thought I needed her assistance. Many times, in the life of a TCK someone will assume, and be very wrong. "About one-in-four (24%) have felt annoyed because people have made assumptions about their racial background."[1]

Opposite of the court translator, I am often told by parishioners that they "don't see color." Most people who make this statement are trying to irrevocably distance themselves from racism, and I appreciate that sentiment.[2] Some articulate colorblindness because they believe that it gives equal benefits to minorities.[3] But, as my friend Kirk Kirkland rightly stated, "colorblindness is a defect!" I much prefer when someone articulates a love of/ affinity for different cultures. An example might be, "Hey what's your ethnic background, for I love learning about people's background!" In this statement one opens up the reality that ethnic backgrounds do have impact upon a person and should be appreciated not avoided.

The phrase "I don't see color" is to "whitewash" someone of their God-given unique background. When one overlooks a person's background you assume many things concerning the person, and the TCK often takes the statement "I don't see color" as disrespect of their minority parent/ family. While one should never make assumptions concerning anyone, an assumption concerning a TCK parishioner can ruin your chances of properly ministering to and later empowering them in the church. The aim of this chapter is to introduce you to the home, head, and heart of the TCK so as to lay the groundwork for the ministerial application in chapters 3 and 4. Throughout this chapter I will also share some conversations I have had with fellow TCKs, concerning these topics.

TCKs Interviewed and Integrated

Peter Yu: Chinese white, Atlanta, GA
Molly L'Hoste: Mexican white, New Orleans, LA
Charles Seville: Japanese white, Houston, TX
Jordan and Kylie Berry: Creole white, Baton Rouge, LA
Kirk Kirkland: Black white, Dayton, OH
Lee Brand: Black white, Memphis, TN

HOME

The first area to discuss is the TCK's home life. In the discussion of home, there are two homes to understand: first is their parents' and second is their own. Regardless of where one is brought up, the parents' home has great impact upon the TCK. The reality of having parents of different ethnicities and cultures can be a wonderful experience and it can also bring about heartache when trying to fit in with friends or with each parent's respective culture. When discussing one's home life I have utilized several questions to help understand the TCK's homelife impact and in the case of those interviewed, these questions have yielded very similar answers.

How have people viewed you and how does it make you feel?
Was angst given toward your family or your parents?
Did your household tend toward one or the other cultural norm?

Reflections on Home

Was angst given toward your family or your parents?
    One of the most anxiety-causing questions to a mixed kid is, "Where are you from?" My wife was once asked where I was from, to which she responded, "Baton Rouge," for I was raised there. The person asked again, "Yea but where is he from?" She responded, "well his family is from New Orleans." Again, "no . . . where is he from," "you mean what ethnicity is he?" "Yes." When one considers a TCK there are dozens of questions posed that the answer does not fit the question.

Understanding a TCK's homelife will vary depending upon two factors, the era they grew up in and the region they grew up in. Growing up I always knew that my family was different because I didn't look like my mom, for she is Caucasian. Being in Baton Rouge as a little child, I never really felt angst toward my parent's marriage. For a TCK raised during the civil rights era, or post–World War II era their homelife probably suffered much. My friend Dr. Charles Seville recalled angst shown toward his parent's marriage because his mother was Japanese, and the era was postwar. As a result of this angst Charles has no connectivity with his Japanese side and identifies as a white male, though he appears quite Asian. My father, who was raised in 1950s–1960s New Orleans had to deal with angst toward my grandparents' marriage for my grandfather was an immigrant and dark brown, and my grandmother was Cajun French. As a result, they were sometimes not permitted into establishments as a family. For others who have a black and white parent structure, they possibly suffered the most depending on the location and the era. Kirk Kirkland recalled his parents' struggle to be accepted because even in Dayton, Ohio, there was segregation and his parents broke the cultural norm. He noted, "we didn't have a railroad that separated the races, but there was a street and my parents crossed it."

I wish that these stories of pain were things of the past. Sadly, the racial angst toward mixed marriages lives on today. "The [Pew] survey finds that many multiracial adults, like other racial minorities, have experienced some type of racial discrimination, from racist slurs to physical threats, because of their racial background."[4] I recall the first date my girlfriend, now wife, and I went on in Memphis. Walking down Main Street to a nice sushi joint we were approached by an older man who looked Bekah straight in the eyes and said, "you know you're not supposed to be with him!" I am grateful for my father's lessons of how he dealt with such hateful speech growing up in New Orleans, "Don't get angry or hate them, they are just articulating what sin would have them say. Pray for them to accept the Gospel." Remembering dad's words, I looked at our confronter and said, "thank you sir, have a good night." Sadly, these ignorant views do invade church psyche at times. Kirk Kirkland told me that he had to get permission to date someone of a different ethnicity when he attended Crown College, a small Christian college in Tennessee, though he himself was mixed. In a similar way, many churches may not confront biracial couples from the pulpit, but you often hear the parishioners questioning teens and young adults as to why they're dating ____ type of a person.

Another struggle that current TCK's and mixed marriages encounter is that of minority preservation. My former judo student Peter Yu, who grew up in Atlanta, recalled his parents' struggles to be accepted not from the white community but rather from the Chinese community. As research shows, "Multiracial individuals are more likely to encounter disapproval and discrimination from their extended families, neighborhoods, and larger communities."[5] Aligning with this research, Peter noted that the Chinese community desired to preserve their culture and race, thus intermarrying was forbidden and could result in excommunication. Peter was even in recent told by the Chinese community to "stop messing around with white girls." Similarly, I remember the day my workout partner in Memphis randomly stated, "I'm worried my girls won't find husbands." To which I asked what on earth he was talking about. He responded, "all these young black guys are marrying white girls, so who will my daughters [who are black] marry?" My previously mentioned friend Matt often receives similar remarks toward his marriage. Because his wife Glenda is Salvadorian, Matt is often told by Hispanic men, "if you white guys keep marrying our Hispanic women who will we marry?" Complicating the mixed Hispanic marriages, friends, like Matt, are often accused of marrying their spouse so they could get citizenship.

All of these stories paint the picture of hurt for most mixed marriages and the children raised within them. Sometimes the TCK will not suffer with a bad upbringing but may suffer later in their personal marriage, as I have. The spectrum of responses to these mixed marriages can be found in both majority and minority cultures. So constantly recall there are probable raw spots when it comes to how their parents' or their marriage is culturally viewed.

Feelings of Home

How have people viewed you and how does it make you feel?

When one reflects upon how they were personally viewed, there is a full spectrum of responses, depending on the situation and the appearance of the TCK. If there is any heartache when reflecting upon the TCK's parents, there is indeed heartache in how the TCK has been viewed.[6] I recall as a young boy someone asking me if my mom was my babysitter, for I'm brown and she's very white. I at times laughed at the question, and at other times cried inside because I wanted it to be evident that she is my mom. In general, there are four ways that a TCK can be viewed: a white majority, a minority, a poser, or a mutt.

Not every TCK looks like a minority person. My sweet friends Kyle and Jordan Berry are a mix of white and Creole. If you know to look at their eyes, you'd see the Cajun Creole hazel and immediately know they're part Creole. However, as Jordan said, her skin tone and hair are that of a white girl. As a result of her appearance, Jordan is most of the time called/viewed as a white majority. The family even jokes and calls her "the white one." A TCK who is viewed as being white will accept the review for it is half true. But the instant classification is a gut wrenching one for most TCK's will have a heart desire to relate to the minority culture. "I am not ashamed of being white, I just want credit for the whole of me!" Jordan is often labeled and viewed as white, yet mentally speaking has cultural preferences equal to minority culture.

Kyle Berry, Jordan's sister, has the same cultural makeup yet looks Creole. She has darker skin tone, what she calls "black girl hair," and her speech pattern is more akin to the minority side of the family. Because of her appearance Kyle is most of the time viewed as a minority and treated as such.[7] This result is in keeping with recent research: "Multiracial adults with a black background—69% of whom say most people would view them as black or African American."[8] While Kyle's classification of being a minority is often what TCKs desire, a full relegation leads to massive misunderstanding and cultural insensitivities.

> Overall, biracial adults who are both white and black are three times as likely to say they have a lot in common with people who are black than they do with whites (58% vs. 19%). They also feel more accepted by blacks than by whites (58% vs. 25% say they are accepted "very well") and report having far more contact with their black relatives: 69% say they've had a lot of contact with family members who are black over the course of their lives, while just 21% report similar levels of contact with their white relatives. About four-in-ten (41%) say they have had no contact with family members who are white. By contrast, biracial adults who are white and Asian say they have more in common with whites than they do with Asians (60% vs. 33%) and are more likely to say they feel accepted by whites than by Asians (62% vs. 47% say they are accepted "very well"). More also say they have had a lot of contact with family members who are white than say the same about Asian members of their family (61% vs. 42%).[9]

I and my brother relate well to Kyle's story. When one reads my name or sees me in person I am immediately classified as a Hispanic minority, though not really and culturally relegated to that population. The result of such relegation is that my brother and I have undoubtedly been overlooked for ministerial positions, or in Mateo's case not been given the opportunity to take the positions which he was serving as interim. This is the exact problem that President Obama noted. Until his presidency no mixed person, on the national level, had broken the cultural system of only fitting into one census box. Thus, he was and by and large still is relegated to being "black." Yet, if you read and listen to the president you will quickly find that he does not fit neatly into the black cultural box.

The result of either of the two previous views is that the TCK is often viewed as being a "poser." When a "white" TCK interacts with white majority culture they are often quickly noted as not being one of them and as a kid/high schooler will encounter harsh jokes about being different. The differences are often subtle, but culturally stick out like a sore thumb. Though I have a minority appearance I experienced this heartache. The majority of my friends growing up were white guys, but I was always labeled different. For instance, most of my high school buddies called me their "favorite Mexican." I have spent significant time in Mexico and helped translate on a dozen mission trips there, but I am not Mexican. Thus, the joke was received with respect toward Mexico and my Mexican friends but was tiresome for I was in no part Mexican. When a minority-appearance TCK interacts with minority culture they too are quickly noted as not being one of them and are often called a poser, for they do not "fully understand the minority struggle." The minority struggle for most of my generation in my family comes from the Filipinos. Without fail when I explain my heritage to an Asian, especially a full Filipino, they will start speaking in Tagalog to me. After explaining that my generation doesn't speak Tagalog they'll usually reply with, "oh . . . I see, you're not really Filipino."

I personally think that being viewed as a poser is the most difficult view to accept and it causes the most emotional heartache. If we TCKs were honest with ourselves, we often feel like posers in most situations. Being Filipino, Spanish, and French has availed opportunities for me to work in white, Asian and Spanish churches. While some of these churches did their best to accept me, after the heritage conversation, I always felt that I was a poser. I was never "Asian enough," "Spanish enough," or "white enough." While the poser view of outsiders hurts, the inner feeling of being a poser hurts all the more for we hear our thoughts continually, versus the brief interactions with others.

Once the TCK has explained their heritage and culture to someone they will most likely be viewed as a mulatto. In American colloquialisms we're classified as a mutt. Sadly, when outsiders come to this conclusion they'll often reply, "As Americans we're all mutts." I understand that the person is trying to show empathy but being a mix of European backgrounds does not bring about the same heart/cultural struggle that a minority-European person suffers with. Being labeled as a mutt can be difficult to accept, but in truth should be accepted because God is uniquely gifting us with capabilities that a mono-ethnic person often doesn't have. A TCK can also be a linguistic/cultural mismatch. My friend Matt's "whiter" daughter prefers everything in Spanish: church, TV, and conversations. In contrast, Matt's "brown" daughter prefers everything in English: church, TV, and conversations. The title of mutt is a very common colloquialism in the United States, and with it comes the hurt of being a "less than desirable" person just as the mutt is less than desirable in the pound. As one who cares for and ministers to TCKs you must constantly be aware of this "less than desirable" attitude toward the TCK and the probability that it has engrained itself into the TCK's psyche.

Through healthy conversations with the TCK one can learn of possible heartache within the TCK. Furthermore, healthy conversations with the TCK can help you avoid "trigger remarks" that lead to such hurtful views. By understanding these "pitfalls" of views, you can help guard and protect the heart of the TCK.

CULTURE WARS AT HOME

Did your household tend toward one or the other cultural norm in the cultural chart?

All TCK's deal with culture wars in their respective homes (see table 2.1). My TCK friends and I love to tell stories of cultural issues in our homes because for us, these issues are most of the time hilarious! A funny in my family is my Filipino side's constant requirement of fresh hot rice with every meal. My grandfather even put hot white rice with his ice cream, and now I love it too! These cultural struggles can be language, food, emotions, gender roles, or time differences. As shown in in table 2.1, there are varying responses to numerous topics.

Most of my surveyed friends were raised in a singular cultural household though their parents were a mixed marriage. When a household is primarily one or the other culture, there are often counter-cultural elements to be found. The primary result of TCKs being raised in a one-sided household is that the TCK is often devoid of cultural knowledge for one of the respective backgrounds. The moments of counter-cultural elements often lead the TCK to have a longing or heart affinity for the lesser seen culture. Molly L'hoste summarized this feeling best, "we always have emotional sadness for not knowing family or cultural backgrounds." In my household, one of the common counter-cultural elements is our Filipino food. The cuisine, for us, is a

Table 2.1 Culture Chart

Majority Culture/Church Culture	*Topic*	*Minority Cultures/Church Culture*
Self	Survival Concern	Community
Personal Control	Control of Life	Fate of God
Tasks	Concern at Gatherings	Human Interaction
Immediate	Family	Extended
Younger Generations	Generational Leadership	Elder Generations
Reserved	Emotion	Expressive
Designated/Patriarchal	Gender Roles	Flexible/Matriarchal
Linear/Organized	Communication	Integrated/Responsive
Direct	Conflict Resolution	Indirect

Source: Adapted from Ernvik, *Third Culture Kids*, 136–37.

glimpse into our Filipino heritage and always leaves me desiring a full grasp of my Filipino side.

When a household is an even mix, via mom and dad behaving differently with most areas, the child tends to be more adept to the two cultural norms. However, a household that has an "even mix" is often a very contentious household. Molly L'hoste remembered that any time something went wrong her parents would blame each other's cultural background. Likewise, I have seen mixed marriages that try to be an "even mix" end up in years of marriage counseling. I have seen dozens of these very marriages end in divorce for the cultural wars were irreconcilable. The fallout of the culture wars can often lead the TCK to lack a good picture of marriage, or home life. Establishing the reality of culture wars is necessary because it determines how the minister will engage and encourage the TCK. Regardless of type of cultural war in the household, every TCK needs cultural encouragement to better walk into one of their respective cultures.

But why is it that so many mixed marriages end up being one sided? In the nineteenth to early twentieth century, America was often labeled as a "melting pot." This term signified that many nations/cultures came to America but then shed their homeland's norm and became American linguistically and culturally speaking. Those that immigrated or were born during this "melting pot" phase of American were often told to only speak English and that cultural norms of the homeland had to be quelled for you didn't want to be labeled. Furthermore, those that immigrated during this time came to the United States to "become American." Thus, my father's generation was told not to speak in Tagalog or French because they were American! The result is that my father is not culturally Filipino, though he has some cultural tendencies.

In the middle of the twentieth century America became what is known as a "salad bowl."[10] The term "salad bowl" signifies that immigrants were indeed in the same place but maintained their unique nature. The "salad bowl effect" truly began in World War II era and became the normal immigration mentality during the Vietnam War era. Contrasting the "melting pot," "salad bowl" immigrants came to the United States not to become American, but to seek asylum, or better opportunities. In the salad bowl, there is little concern for American cultural norms or even American politics. In New Orleans East there is little Vietnam. Thousands of Vietnamese immigrated to that area during the war period. The salad bowl effect has taken such root there that we often say that someone can be born, raised, and can die in New Orleans East only knowing Vietnamese and Vietnamese culture. Throughout the country other national enclaves exist similar to little Vietnam in New Orleans East.

The melting pot and salad bowl effects will have great sway upon the TCK's household. As will be seen in the next section, even those raised in a melting pot mentality now desire to regain their cultural knowledge and background and as a result be in the salad bowl.

TCK's Home

Who did you marry? What culture is in your home?

As the TCK matures they will be faced with choosing who they will marry, and what the culture of their home will be. Though not a formal broad study, I have observed that most TCK's marry someone from American white culture. One notable exception would be President Obama. All but one the TCKs interviewed for this work, married a white person, Lee Brand is the exception. Bolstering this observation, three generations of my family have married someone white. I suspect two things are at play. (1) White culture is the most predominate culture pictured in media. Possibly what is most familiar to us leads us to marry people from white culture.[11] (2) Psychology may actually prove that an interracial person is more desirable for mono-ethnic peoples. Not only does the TCK possibly desire to marry a white person, but the white person may subconsciously desire to marry a mixed person! Four major psychological surveys have been accomplished in recent years concerning appearances and psychological preferences. Interestingly all four have shown a greater preference for the mixed person pictured. One of these studies offered a plausible biological reason for this preference.

> In a 2005 study, Japanese and white Australians found the faces of half-Japanese, half-white people the most attractive, compared with those of either their own race or other single races.
>
> White college students in the UK, meanwhile, were shown more than 1,200 Facebook photos of black, white, and mixed-race faces in a 2009 study and rated the mixed-race faces the most attractive. Only 40 percent of the images used in the study were of mixed-race faces, but they represented nearly three-quarters of those that made it into the top 5 percent by attractiveness rating.
>
> More recently, a 2018 study by psychologists Elena Stepanova at the University of Southern Mississippi and Michael Strube at Washington University in St. Louis found that a group of white, black, Asian, and Latino college students rated mixed-race faces the most attractive, followed by single-race black faces.
>
> A 2005 study led by psychologist Craig Roberts at Scotland's University of Stirling, however, supports the hybrid vigor hypothesis—that genetic diversity makes people more attractive by virtue of their "apparent healthiness."
>
> A 2012 study by Jennifer Patrice Sims, a sociologist at the University of Alabama in Huntsville, found that in general, mixed-race people were perceived as more attractive than people of one race.[12]

As introduced in the previous section, when it comes to determining culture within the TCK's home there is more intentionality to diversity than in the parent's home. "Today's mixed-race parents are more likely to have talked to their own children about being multiracial. Fully 46% of multiracial parents say they talked to their adult children when they were growing up about having a mixed-race background. By contrast, about a third (32%) say their parents had similar conversations with them."[13] Our experiences and sensitivity to the difficulty of being mixed leads us to helping make it easier for our children.

Ways that diverse culture is often integrated are in food, entertainment, and aversion to divisive views. Someone once told me the best way to learn a culture is through your stomach. My parents' house alternated between Cajun, Filipino, and American classical food. My personal love of the three has continued into my marriage, and I have also expanded into more Latin favorites. Now, we rarely eat American standards, but prefer international cuisine given the option.

I grew up in a bilingual home (English and sign language), but I had no real connectivity to our Tagalog, Spanish, and French linguistic roots. To correct this linguistic shortfall, I have learned Spanish and am becoming functional in French. As a means of diversifying my household I alternate languages for video and musical entertainment. Advancements in internet media have provided an ease of such integration. With the flip of a switch I can watch video in Spanish, French, or English. In New Orleans we have locally broadcasted English, Spanish, and alternating French channels to watch. As a musician, I have intentionally expanded my love into Latin Jazz, and French Jazz, and I have retained my love of New Orleans Jazz and classic rock. Not only has my jazz preferences diversified, but also my worship music has linguistically diversified. Groups such as Hillsong now have records in English, Spanish, and French. These familiar songs aid one in learning the language and they serve as the foray into culturally unique worship groups, such as Marcos Witt, Jesus Adrian Romero, and so on.

Most importantly as a TCK I have a massive aversion to divisive topics and one-sided views in my household. Because the TCK has walked between worlds, they will desire for the two sides to be respected and represented. As will be discussed later, TCKs are more linguistically conscientious because of the desire to respect and articulate cultures correctly. The result of a TCK avoiding divisive topics is that we are often labeled as being a sellout, liberal, or conservative. A mixed friend of mine articulated the aversion quite well, "I'm too liberal for my conservative friends and I'm too conservative for my liberal friends."

The minister of a TCK must be aware of the cultural sensitivity of the TCK for in premarital counseling and normal pastoral care issues will arise where the mono-ethnic spouse will struggle to understand the TCK's counter-cultural moments. But, the difficulty of the TCK's marriage can be an asset, for the TCK will probably be able to speak into the life and marriage of minority and majority marriages better than a mono-ethnic pastor can.

Questions for Conversations

TCK:

- How have people viewed you and how does it make you feel?
- Was angst given toward your family or your parents?
- Did your household tend toward one or the other cultural norm?
- What are some funny and not so funny cultural abnormalities at home?

Minister/Parent and TCK:

- What was your (minister/parent) cultural home life like?
- What is your understanding of minority home culture?
- What aspects of opposing home cultures do you struggle to accept and why?
- How should you adapt your ministry to couples when understanding that they have a mixed home?
- What key insight did you glean from this section? And how do you plan to integrate the insight into your life/ministry?

HEAD

The second area to discuss is the TCK's thinking, that is, their "head." Where the discussion of home helps one grasp the social impacts upon the TCK, studying the "head" of the TCK avails the thought process of the mixed person. When one is brought up with parents from different ethnicities and cultural backgrounds the TCK naturally develops a mixed thought process. The impact of such a mixing in the head is a broader understanding of the world, but a later maturation.

Like the study of the home life, several questions can help one understand the TCK's thinking.

When considering the cultural chart, which side do you tend most relate to?
Do you, or have you fluctuated on any of these points?
What impact did your mixed nature have upon your maturation?
Do you think you were more or less mature?

How do you interact with others?
Do you believe that you adapt well, and if so what impact does that have upon your life?

Finding Our Culture

When considering the cultural chart (table 2.1), which side do you tend most relate to? Do you, or have you fluctuated on any of these points?

I find myself to be an even mix of the cultural norms on both sides. Also, the preference changes depending on my situation. As a chameleon I find myself to reflect the cultural norm of the current situation. However, I have a distinct preference on each point. In surveying my TCK friends, I have found that though they were raised in a mono-cultured home, they personally are flexible on the cultural chart. What is interesting when discussing these preferences, we all will give an answer from the head, that which is expected of us. Yet, when talking with a fellow TCK we will reveal our actual preference.

Maturation in Our Culture

What impact did your mixed nature have upon your maturation? Do you think you were more or less mature?

Growing up I was always told that I was "an old soul." Lee Brand's grandparents called him an "old head." I have always preferred friends who were older than me. Yet, in reality, I matured much later than the majority of my actual peers. In surveying my TCK friends they all agreed with my personal observation. As Pollock and Van Reken noted, TCKs have an early maturation and a delayed adolescence.[14] Here's what I suspect is going on.

Because we are raised in a different type of household, we are often asked more serious questions at a young age. (What are you? Where are you from? Why don't you look like your parent?) As a result of this questioning, we are forced to think through our personal and family dynamics long before our peers. Also due to our household we have to defend our personhood much sooner than others further pushing our early maturation. Hearing both sides of the coin, as it were, concerning cultural issues forces a young TCK to think through and broaden their world view at a young age.

Yet, we go through a delayed adolescence, or as I say a longer adolescence, because we have to work through so much more cultural milieu to determine who we are. Peter Yu noted that his communication skills developed later than his peers. He thinks that the possible reason was the Asian family dynamic. Minority families as previously noted are elder led, thus the children in the family take longer to get to a place of independence and self-realization than majority-culture children. Where the mono-ethnic kid can accomplish this adolescent arc within a few years, I and my friends believe that the TCK takes at least eight years to complete adolescence. This longer adolescence results in our friends or outsiders stating that we are "so immature." My friends and I all agree that our adolescence didn't come to an end until we finished college and had our first real career.

Understanding early maturation and yet longer adolescence comes to the fore when considering how to minister to a TCK. They may seem mature and need less attention, yet in reality they need more attention and help thinking through life topics. Whatever you do, do not mention to the TCK "old soul, mature for your age, or immature for your age." If these views are evident to you, they probably are not evident to the TCK for they have not worked through these difficulties and as a result your statement will cause the TCK to think you don't respect them. More on how to accomplish the task of pastoring this conundrum will come in chapter 3.

Interacting Outside Our Culture

How do you interact with others? Do you believe that you adapt well, and if so what impact does that have upon your life?

Several years into coaching judo at Union University one of my senior students looked at me and said, "Mario, you are the whitest guy that I know!" My wife heard this and laughed. For several weeks I took him to a different cultural side of Memphis and the respective restaurant. At the end of each excursion he looked at me and said, "you're the most ____ ethnicity ___ that I know!" This type of cultural blending in is why I consider myself a chameleon TCK.

The diverse upbringing of the TCK forces the TCK to constantly interact outside their culture. According to Pollock and Van Reken, TCKs are more adept to interacting with people of varying backgrounds because they themselves are constantly interacting with people different from themselves.[15] As a result, the TCK will always be more adept to interacting with various people than a mono-ethnic person. They will adapt quickly and be able to articulate correctly in the given situation. Benefits of being a TCK which factor into cross-cultural contact are adaptability, blending in, less prejudice, observational skills, social skills, linguistic skills, large number of relationships, and deep valued relationships.

As TCKs we are labeled as less prejudice than most mono-ethnic people, thus further aiding our interactions.[16] By being half and half, we can empathize with majority and minorities even if they are not the cultures within our families. As a result, TCKs often try to "stand in the gap" and help others think correctly about different people. As Jordan Berry said, "I always felt pride with mixed responsibility. I felt it was my job to help people understand the world through a mixed person's perspective. So, some have perceived this to be arrogance, but I have a perspective and duty to help others understand!" According to the Pew Research, "one-in-five (19%) say that they have felt like they were a go-between or "bridge" between different racial groups."[17]

Sadly, the adaptability that allows us to be less prejudice will often be viewed from the outside as being "more prejudice." As the interviewed TCKs noted, because we don't fully take on and articulate the views of majority or minority cultures, we get labeled by those cultures as being prejudice. Once again, the term often ascribed is "sellout." I recall numerous conversations with friends who were discussing political stances and parties. After articulating a sympathy for both sides and by articulating the pros and cons of each, my friends immediately called me a "liberal or conservative sellout." My minority friends always want me to fully accept and articulate the Democratic progressive views. Yet, I and my TCK friends will rarely fully accept the political and cultural idealistic views of one party over another.

Another aid to TCK interactions with others is our observational and social skills. The elements that brought about heartache for us growing up now empowers us to observe a situation and to integrate into that situation. In essence, we are more sensitive to other's feelings in the very areas we were hurt. However, our observational social skills sometimes are perceived as arrogance. The TCK has experienced life in multiple realms and thinks on a more "global scale."[18] If the TCK is not careful in how they articulate this knowledge they will be called "less approachable" as Kirk Kirkland noted. In spite of this issue, the TCK's observation and social interaction ability has made TCKs highly sought after in corporate leaderships and diplomatic positions.[19]

Finally, the mixed nature of the TCK comes to bare in linguistic capabilities in situations. I am not saying that every TCK speaks multiple languages, though most of us do, the linguistic capability is the careful articulation and speech pattern. The previously mentioned observational and social skills are most evident in the TCKs speech. More than likely a TCK will be much more sensitive to culturally divisive terms, words, and topics than someone who was raised in a mono-ethnic household. The review of the TCK, who has properly utilized their linguistic skills, will be that of "clear" "compassionate" "connective" speech.

Questions for Conversations

TCK:

- When considering the cultural chart, which side do you tend most relate to?
- Do you, or have you fluctuated on any of these points?

- What impact did your mixed nature have upon your maturation?
- Do you think you were more or less mature?
- How do you interact with others?
- Do you believe that you adapt well, and if so what impact does that have upon your life?

Minister/Parent and TCK:

- How would you (minister/parent) categorize your TCK on these charts?
- Does understanding maturation of a TCK give you an aha regarding your TCK?
- In what ways can a TCK be aided in this maturation process?
- What pitfalls exist if the TCK is improperly handled in their maturation and cultural development?
- What key insight did you glean from this section? And how do you plan to integrate the insight into your life/ministry?

HEART

The topics of the TCK's home and head are best summarized in discussing the heart. While some may consider the topic of heart to be redundant of the head, I consider the heart to be the center of one's being and emotion versus the head which is the logic and choice mechanism. Here in the discussion of the TCK's heart one truly can grasp the unique nature of the TCK, especially when considering church ministries. While the TCK can make a choice of blending into a situation or church, the heart is what causes the TCK to feel uncomfortable or even alien within a context. Furthermore, it is the heart of the TCK that breaks when someone refuses to recognize their unique ethnic mix. Four questions can possibly help to understand the TCK's true difficulty of relating and fitting into a situation.

Do you often feel rootless or restless?
What emotion(s) do you feel about your mixed background?
How do you feel in church?
What do you wish ministers would know or do to better minister to the TCK?

Finding Home

Do you often feel rootless or restless?

My friend Molly L'Hoste once said that as a TCK we are "comfortably restless." What she perfectly articulated is that we never feel at home, yet that restlessness is our home. If we remain still in a context too long, we feel that a part of us is dying. Thus, the TCK has a constant desire to relate to multiple cultures more adequately. My brother told me that his move, post college, to Miami truly helped him rest in his minority nature for there in Miami he could somewhat blend in. Yet, truth be told Miami doesn't reflect all aspects of our cultures thus Mateo probably felt a constant lack in one area or another. I spent two summers in Mexico at the end of high school. These summers acted the same way for me as Miami did for Mateo. However, constantly working in Spanish and not seeing white or Asian folks walking about left me feeling lonely. The TCK will never truly feel at home, thus the constant feeling of restlessness. Sarah Gaither, a social psychologist at Duke University says, "Multiracials face the highest rate of exclusion of any group. They're never black enough, white enough, Asian enough, Latino enough."[20] Until the TCK becomes comfortable with who they are, restlessness will result in "years of loneliness" as Peter Yu said.

Emotional Home in Culture

What emotion(s) do you feel about your mixed background? (Have you progressed through?)

When a TCK grows up they seem to work through a progression of feelings. All of my friends I have interviewed for this work completely agreed concerning this progression.

Progression of Feelings Being Mixed

Love → acceptance → confusion → insecurity → hatred → defiance → empowerment

At the heart of this progression is the question, "How have people viewed you and how does it make you feel?" A TCK will not be able to give you one answer for this question, because they are constantly moving on this progression of feelings.

> Racial identity can be fluid and may change over the course of one's life, or even from one situation to another. About three-in-ten adults with a multiracial background say that they have changed the way they describe their race over the years—with some saying they once thought of themselves as only one race and now think of themselves as more than one race, and others saying just the opposite.[21]

What I have found is that a grown TCK may not fully accomplish this progression but may remain in one of the phases, thus explaining some of the

TCK states in the previously mentioned animal paradigm. Furthermore, a move of location, or a major change in life can force the TCK to revert to a previous stage.

As a little child, we love our mixed nature, for it is all that we know. When someone asks, "Is that your mom or dad?" I would happily smile and say "YES." We are in the love phase, for we are ignorant to the difference struggle. As we move into elementary school, people will ask what your background is and you become very good at articulating some answer (though not fully correct) and by nature have accepted the difference. "I am Filipino-Cajun." However, as we begin trying to navigate upper elementary to find our friends and place, we become confused because we don't quite fit in. "I have many white friends but don't feel like they get me?" Peter Yu remembered one occasion that broke his heart having to put his name into the computer for class and the whole class laughing at it and then calling him a "chink." Thankfully, Peter had a father who taught him lessons of taking the high road. Peter's dad, though Chinese, was raised in Korea and often got beaten for that fact, but he took the high road and always reminded Peter to do the same.

Junior high and high school will bring about the most anxiety and social pressure. Being a teenager is bad enough, but not being accepted into groups leads the TCK to constantly feel insecure, whether or not they articulate such. I felt that being mixed was no longer a good answer for I was the only mixed kid, yet that is what I was! Insecurity leads to hatred of one's nature in high school when kids are the most closed minded, because you will look at a student who you look similar to, yet they won't welcome you to their lunch table. I recall my first day at my Pentecostal high school, the Asians, Hispanics, and white tables wouldn't welcome me to sit. So, I sat with the black guys. Interestingly, most of the TCK friends surveyed likewise built up black friendships in this stage of life. I think I felt some sort of hatred and envy for those other groups because I wanted to be their friend and wanted to bounce between all of them. Peter Yu suffered in the same way at lunch and was accused of eating worms because he'd bring LoMein to school for lunch.

College brings about a new dawn and a season of defiance. The days of being relegated to the outcast table are gone and you can re-label yourself to be whoever you choose. This choice is called defiance because as an adult we are often pressured to choosing who we are. "According to the survey, about one-in-five (21%) say they have felt pressure from friends, family or 'society in general' to identify as a single race."[22] My first year at Samford University was spent hanging out with all the Hispanic students and speaking in Spanish, I even served as a Spanish youth intern at a local church. However, I felt strange and like a poser by looping myself into just one group. Thus, as one navigates through defiance and choosing who you will be, you suddenly come to the point of not only accepting your unique difference but feeling empowered by it. I remember my guidance counselor at Leavell College asked my ethnicity and then encouraged me to be honest because it was an asset to me and any organization I worked with! At Leavell and Union University my diversity was encouraged, and I was given the opportunity to serve in English, Spanish, and Asian churches whenever I was free. Post college is truly the season where you are empowered as a mixed person to fulfill unique roles, and places. During grad school I was further encouraged to walk into the various ethnic ministry circles, and I was constantly asked to come and speak on diversity and diversifying churches. Suddenly that which relegated you as a child → high schooler is your ticket to better employment opportunities.

Yet, if a TCK stops on one of the other phases and doesn't work all the way through the spectrum, they will either be constantly disgruntled, or they may just ignore portions of their true selves. My friends who I interviewed related so strongly to this paradigm, that several realized they were stuck and needed to continue pushing to get to the end where they could be a better TCK for the sake of the church. For a more in-depth corroborating study on the social engagement and psychology of multiracial identity, see Binning et al.'s work.[23]

Church ≠ My Home

How did you feel growing up in church?

Understanding the heart of the TCK in the church is the crux for the remainder of this book. As previously noted, I have never felt at home in any church. My friends that I interviewed always felt that their respective church did not feel like home for there was always an uncomfortable cultural balance. Three main areas determine the comfortability of the TCK in a church: leadership, gender roles, and style.

As Pollock and Van Reken noted TCKs are often mistrustful of leadership.[24] I believe a mistrust of leadership comes from the TCKs home culture. Some TCKs hold a particular view of certain ethnicities and even ages when it comes to leadership. I know numerous of my Filipino and Spanish friends and family that do not trust a pastor who has not seen "the majority of the congregation born." Most minority churches, like minority culture, reserve leadership positions for elders in the community. Thus, I as a thirty-something pastor rarely garner their respect. By contrast, some majority cultured TCKs do not hold much respect for the elder pastor for they are "antiquated, outdated, or out of touch." At all the schools I attended the people talked about, lifted up, and praised as the pastors to listen to/imitate were young white ministers. While outliers existed in these lists (such as John Piper, or

Tim Keller), the majority thought that the pastor who had been in the pulpit for thirty-plus years did not understand or know how to pastor the up and coming generations. Thus, they were not in the conversation and were rarely given admiration.

Another reason a TCK may not feel comfortable in your church is the view/empowerment of genders. Churches tend to divide concerning gender roles. By and large, minority cultures tend to be matriarchal. While most minority churches do have a male pastor, there is strong place of leadership for females in the church. Molly L'Hoste reflected that when she became a believer and began attending a Presbyterian church in New Orleans she was off put and horribly uncomfortable because the women were not represented in leadership of any kind. Contrasting this view, a TCK raised in a majority cultured household probably will feel very uncomfortable with female leadership in a church. While my household was primarily white culture, my family truly tended to be matriarchal. Thus, for me I always want to see both female and male leaders in a church. However, as an Evangelical Baptist, I believe that the head pastor position is preserved for male pastors.

The last reason a TCK may not feel at home is the style choices of the church. I am not only referring to music and clothing choices but cultural style choices. Is your church more community focused or individual focused? Is your church more concerned with human interaction or with checking off the "to do" list of a typical Sunday? Is your church reserved or expressive emotionally speaking? Is your church/pastor more linear in articulation or is he more integrated/responsive? These topics will be further discussed in chapters 3 and 4, but truly show the paradigms which hold sway over a TCK feeling comfortable in a church.

"The Changing Complexion of American Congregations"—published in the *Journal for the Scientific Study of Religion*.[25]

- One-third of U.S. congregations were composed entirely of one race in 2012, down from nearly half of U.S. congregations in 1998.
- Multiracial congregations constituted 12 percent of all U.S. congregations in 2012, up from 6 percent in 1998.
- The percentage of Americans worshipping in multiracial congregations climbed to 18 percent in 2012, up from 13 percent in 1998.
- Mainline Protestant and Evangelical Protestant churches have become more common in the count of multiracial congregations, but Catholic churches continue to show higher percentages of multiracial congregations. One in four Catholic churches was multiracial in 2012.

- While whites are the head ministers in more than two-thirds (70 percent) of multiracial congregations, the percentage of those led by black clergy has risen to 17 percent, up from fewer than 5 percent in 1998.
- Blacks have replaced Latinos as the most likely group to worship with whites. In the typical multiracial congregation, the percentage of black members rose to nearly a quarter in 2012, up from 16 percent in 1998. Meanwhile, Latinos in multiracial congregations dropped from 22 percent in 1998 to 13 percent in 2012.
- The percentage of immigrants in multiracial congregations decreased from over 5 percent in 1998 to under 3 percent in 2012.

What do you wish ministers would know or do to better minister to the TCK?

Before moving into practical ministry applications one last question was posed to my TCK friends. What do you wish ministers to know? I found the answers to this question were uniform in three primary points: don't fake diversity, preach the diversity of the gospel, and allow culture to be genuine.

I know of several churches who espouse the title "multi-ethnic." In truth when you closely examine these churches, the diversity does not fulfill the 80 percent rule. Much of the diversity at these "multi-ethnic" churches come from minority adoptions, not adult inclusion. As one friend said regarding a church, "X church is not multi-ethnic, they just say that they are, so they get attention and praise in a very mono-ethnic church culture." Closer inspection of churches like this one reveal token hires, who rarely remain in ministerial position for more than a couple years. If diversity were genuine then culture would have changed, and minorities would feel comfortable enough to remain. As several of my TCK friends articulated, "we smell fake diversity like a skunk on the road." In my observation TCKs are more sensitive to fake diversity than mono-ethnic people. I am not quite certain why this is the case, but it points toward the need for churches to diversify genuinely. I and my friends interviewed for this work all are suspicious of the church that feels the need to label themselves as multi-ethnic. As one friend said, "A biblically diverse church comes from Gospel preaching to a diverse congregation and gives praise to Christ, not some tag line."

The second common response from my TCKs is that they never heard the gospel's implication on kingdom diversity in the church preached from the pulpit. As stated in the opening of this book, I never heard this element of the gospel preached until I met Bryan Loritts in Memphis. Both minority and majority churches are guilty of this lack of gospel implication in the pulpit. Some pastors spend decades preaching epistles, yet never once highlight the epistle's initial purpose of unifying an ethnically divided church. As Dr. Charles Seville noted,

We as evangelicals have reduced the Gospel to personal salvation. Whereas if you dig a little deeper into the NT there is much more! Reconciliation between you and God and others. There are benefits that come which exceed just forgiveness of sins and "fire insurance." We have flattened the Gospel to its personal effects. When it is all "me and my" there isn't much space for others of another ethnicity.

As mentioned, I found more comfort in my martial arts school than I did at my church, because we were unified for one purpose. Peter Yu reflected that soccer was his outlet for community, for they were a team.

> Multi-ethnicity is not taught because there is no place for it. There's no one in leadership that truly grasps the Gospel implication. And most of all, we too quickly run to identify in Christ, before fully understand what it is Scripture is saying through their own experience. (Molly L'Hoste)

Thus, if you want to make a TCK feel welcomed, preach not only the salvation of man but the unity of the community!

The last response of recommendation for pastors and churches is to let the church culture come about naturally. As Charles Seville noted, "Preach what it means to minister to the community (Rev. 9–13), and remember regardless if we believe it, Revelation will happen!" I have seen churches desire to be multi-ethnic move so fast that they alienate those that currently attend the church. Genuine culture is a culture that is responsive and ministerial to those in the congregation. My church in New Orleans had the opportunity to minister to a diverse neighborhood. However, the church congregation was an older white congregation. While they did not mind the occasional upbeat song, we could not make dynamic changes in culture. But, one summer we had a seminary couple, who were from Zimbabwe, serve as worship leaders. The culture shifted slightly the music changed in pace and everyone there was pleased. In that summer I learned cultural changes that minister to a demographic represented in the church are easier to accept than a "field of dreams" change.

Questions for Conversations

TCK:

- Do you often feel rootless or restless? What is required to help you feel at rest?
- What emotion(s) do you feel about your mixed background? Where are you on the progression of feelings chart?

- How do you feel in church?
- What do you wish ministers would know or do to better minister to the TCK?

Minister/Parent and TCK:

- What place do you think your TCK is on the emotional progression chart?
- What makes you (minister/parent) feel like you belong somewhere?
- How can you help a TCK feel the sense of belonging?
- What are the implications of a TCK not feeling at home in a church?
- How do you (minister) respond to the honest responses from the interviewed regarding what they wish ministers knew to better minister to a TCK?
- What key insight did you glean from this section? And how do you plan to integrate the insight into your life/ministry?

APPLICATION

As seen in this chapter, the TCK in your church has lived a life walking cultural lines. Though they may seem "mature" and "put together," they often have deep cultural heartaches. Though the TCK may be sitting in the pew of the local congregation, they are rarely emotionally connected due to the heartache. What starts with the parent's home affects the heart and head of the TCK. I encourage you to have open conversations with the TCK about how they genuinely feel in church and in culture. Only by hearing their personal feelings can you begin to minister to them appropriately.

SUGGESTED READING

Equally Yoked: A Premarital Counseling Primer for Multiethnic Christian Couples by Matthew Akers.
Mixed Messages: Multiracial Identities in the "Color-Blind" Era edited by David L. Brunsma.
"Resolving Racial Ambiguity in Social Interactions" by Sarah E. Gaither, Laura G. Babbitt, and Samuel R. Sommers.
"Thinking Outside the Box: Multiple Identity Mind-Sets Affect Creative Problem Solving" by Sarah E. Gaither, Jessica D. Remedios, Diana T. Sanchez, and Samuel R. Sommers.
Ministering in Honor-Shame Cultures: Biblical Foundations and Practical Essentials by Jayson Georges and Mark D. Baker.
The 3D Gospel: Ministry in Guilt, Shame, and Fear Cultures by Jayson Georges.

Stages of Biracial Identity Formation: Positive Findings by a Multiracial Doctor by Eve M. Holton.

"Caught in the Middle: Defensive Responses to IAT Feedback among Whites, Blacks, and Biracial Black/Whites" by Jennifer L. Howell, Sarah E. Gaither, and Kate A. Ratliff.

New Perspectives on Racial Identity Development: Integrating Emerging Frameworks, Second Edition, by Jackson Bailey.

Finding Home: Third Culture Kids in the World by Rachel Jones.

The Borders of Race: Patrolling "Multiracial" Identities by Melinda Mills.

Honor and Shame: Unlocking the Door by Roland Muller.

"Patterns of Situational Identity Among Biracial and Multiracial College Students" by Kristen A. Renn.

I'm Chocolate, You're Vanilla: Raising Healthy Black and Biracial Children in a Race-Conscious World by Marguerite Wright.

Chapter 3

Your Ministry for the Third Culture Kid

I have a vivid memory of the day I realized I was the "only" in a church service. I was sitting with a lady we called Grandma Holt, by the deaf section, because mom was down front interpreting. I recall looking around during the song portion, singing with my voice and poorly with my hands while noticing that I was the only brown person in church. Since that first occasion, I have worked at numerous ethnic and linguistic churches where I always have a moment of realization that I am the "only" something there. While my ethnic/cultural makeup is only matched by my brother, I have learned that certain aspects of church can be better tooled to reach the mixed kid and as a result be more welcoming to the mono-cultured parents! In this chapter I propose four areas in which a church can more purposefully minister to the TCK and as a result build a multi-ethnic church: discipleship, service, sensitivity, and preaching.

TC IN DISCIPLESHIP

In the previous chapters I introduced the three questions all Christian TCKs must answer to grasp their diversity. (Why don't I feel comfortable at my church? Who should I listen to? How does the Gospel apply to me?) Furthermore, I stated that the process of answering these questions requires a lifetime of discipleship. But what is discipleship? What examples do we have of such a multi-ethnic relationship? And how does this relationship dovetail into current TCK psychological studies?

What Is Discipleship?

This question has been often discussed for the last few years in the must-read books of church growth.[1] Sadly, none of these books, as far as I know, have connected discipleship with preexisting ideology, especially ideology within minority churches. Some may not highly regard the theology of ethnic churches, but you cannot ignore their community focus and care. Ethnic churches for years have had great success in the area of discipleship and training. What has made them so successful? One simple answer is community focus. When I ask a traditional mainstream white church pastor what their plan is for discipleship, they will usually answer with a "program." When I ask a minority pastor, he often responds with a question, "What do you mean discipleship . . . program? We just . . . live." Programs are useful, and common, but the common community ideology of the minority church member requires a different ideology of discipleship.

Because formal theological education is not common among minority churches, it is only natural for minority believers to teach their beliefs as they go about their lives. This process of discipleship was started because of a couple reasons. (1) Because theological education was not as available to minority church pastors, unlike white church pastors, the minority church did not retain a formal discipleship program for the parishioners. In my experience if the pastor has had formal theological training, they often have a more formal discipleship program for their parishioners. (2) The community was forced to rely upon each other daily due to persecution of numerous kinds. At best there may have been Sunday school, but the regular means of teaching was living life with one another. As a friend of mine says, this is Teologia de la mesa (theology of the table) or Teologia de Abuela (theology of the grandmother), for elder generations often teach younger generations as they went along their way. The shortcoming of such lifestyle discipleship is that not every topic is intentionally discussed, thus there may be voids of knowledge or even worse heretical knowledge developed by the disciple.

Catechisms, classes, and other traditional type classes have been a historic means to discipleship, especially in the majority churches where pastors have advanced theological education. By no means is it wrong to utilize these tools/methods. However, if you only do discipleship in these formats you will develop a great knowledge, but often leave the parishioner without a grasp of Christian living. In the church I pastored in New Orleans, I weekly heard heartbreaking conversations with parents who "raised their child right," and "catechized" their child yet their child is living apart from the Christian faith, and some apart from the family. I do not fault catechism for the lack of Christian faith in these children, but the lack of lifestyle discipleship may have been the cause.

When considering how to disciple a multi-ethnic person, I suggest that it needs to be a harmony of the two views, for they culturally and mentally will respond best to the two unique types of discipleship. For instance, I am very logical and linear in my educational thinking, thus catechism ensured that I knew the full gambit of Christian knowledge. I also have a communal learning preference. Thus, I with a mentor holistically integrated those teachings into my life. Or as Ken said, "put feet to the catechism." From my experience, I have gleaned that some ethnicities need to learn to be more logical on topics covered, and some ethnicities need to learn how to live life together better. I term this mixture as "strategically organic" discipleship. I believe this harmony is the original meaning of discipleship in the Old Testament Hebrew context.

> [18]You shall therefore lay up these words of mine in your heart and in your soul, and you shall bind them as a sign on your hand, and they shall be as frontlets between your eyes. [19]You shall teach them to your children, talking of them when you are sitting in your house, and when you are walking by the way, and when you lie down, and when you rise. [20]You shall write them on the doorposts of your house and on your gates. (Deut. 11:18)

By utilizing this harmony of methods, you will not only speak into the life of a TCK in a way that they best grasp, but I believe this strategic discipleship of the TCK will yield a better holistic discipleship for all believers. The minority parent will appreciate the communal engagement, and the majority parent will appreciate the logical nature of the discipleship. Likewise, modern TCK studies describes what a TCK needs, and somewhat describes a discipleship relationship. "The TCK therefore needs safe adults with whom to process, who understand what it is like to be a TCK. Permission to verbalize and express both what is good and what is not good. Fellow TCKs with whom to share experiences."[2]

Is There a Biblical Example to Follow?

Within the relationship between Timothy and Paul one finds not only the model relationship but an ancient fulfillment of modern TCK studies. As noted before, TCK discipleship is a lifetime process. Paul and Timothy's relationship pictured in scripture is approximately twenty years long. As a result, Paul and Timothy's relationship reveals several lessons that not only give an example for modern TCK discipleship, but perfectly fulfill the modern psychological suggestions of caring for at TCK.

Ways to support TCKs[3]

- Help the TCK have as much ownership over his life as possible—which means to help the TCK understand who he is.
- Help the TCK incorporate/integrate his different cultures/lives into one life story—which means to be aware of and include both gains and losses.
- Help the TCK have a sense of belonging—to himself, to his family, to all the cultures where he has lived, including his passport country—which means being intentional about building and keeping relationships as well as setting up long term goals. (33–34 Ernvik)

The TCK therefore needs

- Safe adults with whom to process, who understand what it is like to be a TCK.
- Permission to verbalize and express both what is good and what is not good.
- Fellow TCKs with whom to share experiences.

Before beginning a relationship, the discipler must understand their role. Paul fulfilled what is now termed as an "anchor" adult, "with whom to process, and verbalize both what is good and what is not good."[4] Paul, a Jew, willingly took Timothy as a disciple, despite the ethnic and cultural issues (Acts 16:1–5). In Acts 16 Paul meets Timothy, who was already a believer, in Lystra. Interestingly the author notes his heritage as such, "the son of a Jewish woman who was a believer, BUT his father was a Greek" (emphasis added). One can see with Luke's word choice "BUT" that there was indeed an ethnic/cultural issue with Timothy's Greek heritage. In response, to the issue Paul circumcises Timothy because the Jews there "knew that his father was a Greek." While circumcision has many theological and cultural implications, for now this action and Luke's word choice of "but" highlights the existing Jewish hesitation toward Timothy's Greek nature.

TIMOTHY, THE THIRD CULTURE KID

Timothy must have been something special, for Paul immediately not only brought him into a discipleship relationship but also utilized him as an assistant. Possibly Timothy's name helped to quell any fears of Paul for Timothy's name means "honoring God" or "precious to God." As one reads through

Timothy's life these two names prove to be an adequate descriptor. More than likely, it was Timothy's mother and grandmother that helped to sway Paul's choosing of Timothy. Lois and Eunice had been among Paul's first converts from the Jewish community in Lystra, and Timothy most likely responded to the gospel between Paul's visits.

When one considers discipling someone, they must make a conscious choice to take on the person as though becoming their surrogate parent, just as Paul did with Timothy. "How as a son with a father he has served with me in the gospel" (Phil. 2:22). Quite possibly Timothy would have never been discipled had Paul not come along and willingly took on a TCK, for the Jews "knew that his father was a Greek." Likewise, I have seen many TCKs overlooked in youth groups, and even adult groups. A probable reason is that disciplers often feel incapable of speaking into their lives, or they worry about crossing a cultural line.

As seen in later stories, Paul in his relationship with Timothy willingly took on this relationship for the sake of the gospel. Discipling a TCK must be intentional and must be for the sake of the gospel! Yes, indeed the person may not become a pastor, but your relationship with the TCK is the gospel at work in their life.

When you intentionally begin a relationship with a disciple, especially a TCK you must learn their life story and their feelings about life. Without a proper understanding of the TCK's experiences and psyche you will inevitably hurt their feelings by articulating something in a "sore spot" of the TCK's life. Thus, as modern TCK studies attest, you must help the TCK debrief. I truly was not able to learn who I was in Christ and my role in the church until a mentor had me articulate my full life story (including my family's) and my emotions regarding numerous topics.

Debriefing is helpful as it[5]

- Offers a space and a place to tell my story.
- Can be a help to process and normalize feelings, thoughts, and behaviors.
- Affirms and validates what I have been through and what I have felt.
- Helps me integrate what I have been through into my life story.
- Helps me to understand my part and role in what has happened and what I am not responsible for.
- Brings in safety to what was scary.
- Offers space to grief unfulfilled expectations.
- Helps to find healthy strategies.
- Brings closure.
- Makes me ready to look at the future.

Not only did Paul willingly begin an anchor relationship with a TCK, but secondly, Paul advocated for Timothy to the churches (1 Cor. 4:16–17, Phil. 2:19–24). Returning to the Acts 16 passage one could understand Paul circumcising Timothy to be the result of some sort of religious peer pressure. However, a common minority reading that I've heard (especially among my Messianic Jewish friends) sees this action as Paul helping Timothy to embrace his culture. It is impossible to know if Timothy grew up faithfully attending synagogue, reading Torah, and having a bar mitzvah. However, the lack of circumcision hints that these were not practices in Timothy's life. Paul's act of circumcision was the discipler helping him "become more Jewish."

Timothy apparently had been a believer from a young age (Acts 16:1; 2 Tim. 1:5), but lacked a full grasp of his Jewish faith. Like many minority believers, Timothy grew up with the faith being modeled by his grandmother, Lois, and his mother, Eunice. The female model and imparting of the faith to Timothy is what we often call Teologia de Abuela. Abuela, or in my case Granny, imparts to us great wisdom of the ages and testimony of God's faithfulness in the good and bad times. However, we can deduce from Timothy's moving to Paul as his discipler that our Abuelas and moms are only a portion of our lifetime of discipleship. The finer points of ecclesiology and theology rarely come from these ladies, but rather come from pastors who take us on like Paul took Timothy under his wing. In my life I have had not only my granny and my mother, but several other ladies left a theological mark on me. In fact, my favorite living biblical studies professor is Dr. Sandra Richter. Another capable woman in my life is my mother-in-law who holds two master's degrees from two different seminaries, thus she is more than capable of fulfilling a discipler role. In Timothy's life however, Lois and Eunice undoubtedly knew that Timothy needed more than they could give.

Like Paul and the circumcision of Timothy, the modern minister of the TCK will need to push the TCK to become more a part of their heritage so as to better grasp that heritage, and to speak into the lives of those who will listen. Reflecting back to the types of TCK (in chapter 1) one can see how almost every noted type could use some encouragement to grow in their heritage and background knowledge. The result in Timothy's case is that he was better equipped to serve those in the Jewish community. Likewise, modern discipleship of a TCK should result in a person being more capable to minister in their respective heritage groups.

Not only did Paul advocate to Timothy to know more of his heritage, but he also advocated on behalf of Timothy to the churches he would minister to (1 Cor. 4:16–17, Phil. 2:19–24). When Paul first met Timothy in Lystra the Jews were skeptical of Timothy. However, once Timothy had been trained, Paul advocated Timothy as not only knowing Paul's teachings but one who was uniquely capable to help churches grow, hence his multiple assignments on behalf of the Apostle.

When a TCK joins a church the discipler has the responsibility to not only educate the disciple in biblical things but advocate for him in the church. As will be discussed later, advocation comes in numerous forms such as reasons for church, types of worship, representation in service, cultural sensitivity in preaching, and opportunities to celebrate different cultural flavors of Christianity. In essence, Paul's relationship with Timothy should inspire ministers to advocate for the third cultured who often do not fully fit into the norm of many churches or organizations.

An anchor person[6] (aka discipler)

- Is a safe base; a safe harbor where I can put my anchor down, attach myself, and rest.
- Is a "gas station" where I can be refueled with love, and knows me and loves me, whatever I do.
- Sees me, tries to understand me and my needs, and tries hard to meet my needs.
- Wants to share my emotions, helps me to understand my emotions, and "harbors" them until I am able to do so myself.
- Helps me, supports me, and makes sure I have what I need.
- Gives me freedom to be myself, but also lets me know that I belong.
- Protects me and makes sure I am safe.
- Is someone I can always return to and find security.

Questions for Conversations

TCK:

- Do you relate to Timothy in that you don't fully relate to one of your ethnic backgrounds?
- Do you innately desire an "anchor person" in your life?
- What exactly do you desire from this person?
- What one thing would you wish an "anchor person" not do when in relationship with you?

Minister/Parent and TCK:

- Were you discipled? If so, what did that look like? What would you change?
- How can you encourage a TCK to grow in their relationship/knowledge of their distinct backgrounds?
- Who are the primary disciplers in your church/ministry? Why do they seem to do the majority of discipleship?

- How can you encourage other people to disciple believers?
- What key insight did you glean from this section? And how do you plan to integrate the insight into your life/ministry?

THREE THEOLOGIES OF DISCIPLING A TIMOTHY

As one considers the preserved teachings of Paul to Timothy, one can grasp three "types" of necessary theology; biblical theology, missional theology, and table theology. These three types of theology helped Timothy to answer the TCK Christian questions and helped Timothy to become the uniquely qualified individual the first-century churches needed.

The first type of theology to consider in discipling Timothy is biblical theology.

> Biblical theology, as defined here, is dynamic not static. That is, it follows the movement and process of God's revelation in the Bible. It is closely related to systematic theology (the two are dependent upon one another), but there is a difference in emphasis. Biblical theology is not concerned to state the final doctrines which go to make up the content of Christian belief, but rather to describe the process by which revelation unfolds and moves toward the goal which is God's final revelation of his purposes in Jesus Christ. Biblical theology seeks to understand the relationships between the various eras in God's revealing activity recorded in the Bible. The systematic theologian is mainly interested in the finished article—the statement of Christian doctrine. The biblical theologian, on the other hand, is concerned rather with the progressive unfolding of truth. It is on the basis of biblical theology that the systematic theologian draws upon the pre-Pentecost texts of the Bible as part of the material from which Christian doctrine may be formulated.[7]

We can possibly infer a holistic biblical theology from Paul's letter to Timothy in 1 Tim. 4:6, "being trained in the words of the faith of the good doctrine that you have followed." Another possibly more explicit picture of Paul's advocation of biblical theology can be found in 2 Timothy 4

> [14]But as for you, continue in what you have learned and have firmly believed, knowing from whom you learned it [15]and how from childhood you have been acquainted with the sacred writings, which are able to make you wise for salvation through faith in Christ Jesus. [16]All Scripture is breathed out by God and profitable for teaching, for reproof, for correction, and for training in righteousness,[17] that the man of God may be complete, equipped for every good work.

Though the term "biblical theology" was invented in 1787, the concept is evident in Paul's teachings to Timothy. Paul throughout his letters and his sermons constantly articulated the story of God (missio dei). In discipleship, Paul was concerned with helping Timothy to know the story of God. As a result of this biblical theology, Timothy developed a focus upon the important points of theology and he developed a holistic understanding of his place in the story.

I accepted the gospel at the age of seven. Mrs. Foy, my first-grade teacher, told us the story of King Arthur and his knights of the round table. Like the other boys, I was enamored with the story. Mrs. Foy wisely took advantage of the teaching moment and told us that Jesus, like King Arthur, is looking for knights to be part of his kingdom and to help grow it/defend it. Of course, I said, I want to be a knight for Christ. Little did I know, Mrs. Foy was articulating what I now know to be biblical theology. "To become part of the Kingdom, you must know what Jesus did for you." The result of that day was that I accepted Jesus not only as savior and sacrifice for my sins, but also as Lord of my life. I have since spent the majority of my educational career studying biblical theology and how to integrate it into all aspects of church life. For the TCK biblical theology helps answer the three TCK questions.

Who Should I Listen To?

Teaching biblical theology aids Timothy to listen to scripture as his truth giver, not just Paul. When one accepts biblical theology, they learn that the whole story and their place in the story is the dictator of life, not just the whim and way of a contemporary society. Such a concept makes me think of Paul's exhortation in Romans 12 of not conforming to this world but being transformed in mind.

My first home church, an independent fundamental Baptist church, in Baton Rouge went through five years of turmoil. This turmoil was caused by ministers falling from grace and leaving the ministry. Affairs, drugs, and theft were rampant in the pastoral staff. The result was that most of the kids in that church dropped out of church and have subsequently left the faith. The initial gospel acceptance via biblical theology, and my parent's constant urge of personalization of my faith helped to bolster my faith though ministers were failing the church.

The TCKs question of who they should listen to is born from mistrust and cultural confusion. I have heard many TCKs ask questions concerning trusting the pastoral staff because they were told or have experienced wrongdoings such as my experience. By utilizing biblical theology to disciple a TCK, the disciple holds tightly to the story and not the minister. As one of my mentors once said, "don't rely and hold onto me. I am man and all men fail at some level."

Why Don't I Feel Comfortable at My Church?

Biblical theology brings about a multi-ethnic understanding of the church which helps to answer this question. In biblical theology one learns that the Kingdom of Christ is much more than one race, style, and language. A friend of mine rightly said, "if we don't espouse biblical theology we can quickly espouse our culture and language as the Gospel of truth." He carried on and reminded us that in earlier missions some said, "Jesus saves and shaves." In essence, the missionaries espoused not only the spiritual nature of the gospel, but also the physical appearance of the European church in that age. Thus, the question of why a TCK doesn't feel comfortable in a church is that the diversity of the gospel is not a reality in the church. So, the mixed kid will always feel out of place for they are not fully representative of the culture.

I don't feel comfortable in most churches, because of the cultural differences, and the often lack of representation (minority or white depending on the situation). This reality in college led me to bemoan the church's practices. When I finally grasped biblical theology as a center to my church thinking, I suddenly felt okay not feeling comfortable in a church. Comfort became secondary or even tertiary to being part of the kingdom. Biblical theology permits the TCK to understand there is no uniform church, and that uniformity is not required. Thus, the mixed kid fits into the church better than they may initially think.

How Does the Gospel Apply to Me?

Biblical theology shows that salvation is no longer for the Jews alone, *though I espouse that it never was*. If it were left up to the Jews in Lystra, Timothy may have remained excluded from "the Jewish people of God," as signified by his lack of circumcision. Yet, when Paul meets Timothy, he welcomes Timothy into the people of Christ, for the church is diverse. Timothy's half Greek side did not exclude him from the new people of God.

I doubt that TCKs feel that they can't be saved, but I bet many TCKs have wondered how the gospel can apply to them when they don't "fit" in the church. For instance, I have heard friends say that they don't "do church," because it is a "white man's thing" or "no thanks that's a brown man's superstition." A proper response is that the gospel is for everyone and you fit into the great story, just as much as the mono-ethnic believer.

Questions for Conversations

TCK:

- Have you ever related your life to the full story of God?
- How does knowing your place in the story of God impact you?

Minister/Parent and TCK:

- As a minister, were you taught to think of a grand story narrative like biblical theology espouses?
- How can your church/family integrate the reality of the story of God?
- What are the implications of not implementing biblical theology?
- What key insight did you glean from this section? And how do you plan to integrate the insight into your life/ministry?

The second type of theology Paul constantly taught to Timothy is missional theology. I do not believe that one can teach biblical theology without subsequently teaching missional theology. In 1 Tim. 4:9–10 Paul reminds Timothy of not only the scriptures (the story of God) but also the reality that Jesus is Savior of all.[9] "The saying is trustworthy and deserving of full acceptance.[10] For to this end we toil and strive, because we have our hope set on the living God, who is the Savior of all people, especially of those who believe." In context, Paul is writing to Timothy to encourage and instruct him in the ministry, and as a result here we see that Paul's biblical theology comes to the reality of missional theology. Timothy is there serving this church and teaching, for it is God's mission to spread the good news to all people!

Missional theology taught to Timothy is found throughout the New Testament and is most evident in Paul's epistles. The epistles of Romans, 1 and 2 Corinthians and Ephesians were all written as a unifying multi-ethnic letter. For instance, a missional theological reading of Romans begins rightly with salvation of the Jews and of the Greeks. The result seen in Romans 12 is that we rejoice with those who rejoice and weep with those who weep. We exalt others over ourselves and seek no vengeance. Thus, the gospel is that Christ died for the covenant people of God and was then subsequently shared with those outside the Jewish community.

Another way Paul taught Timothy missional theology is by taking him on mission trips. I have been on dozens of mission trips in my life. I tell all believers you should go on a mission trip, not for what you can do for the people you visit, but rather what the trip will do to you! Much like the words of Mark Twain, "Travel is fatal to prejudice, bigotry, and narrow-mindedness, and many of our people need it sorely on these accounts." When I went on my first mission trip to Mexico, I learned that the gospel was much larger than my little world of South Louisiana. Furthermore, I learned that the traditions and cultural norms of my church were not the only means of practicing the faith.

Why Don't I Feel Comfortable at My Church?

Missional theology expands the reality of why the church exists, not to preserve the "frozen chosen," but rather to reach "Jerusalem, Judea, Samaria, and the ends of the earth!" By teaching Timothy missional theology and taking Timothy on mission trips Paul helped Timothy to realize that the local parish is just a glimpse into the global eternal church. When I feel uncomfortable in a church setting, I rest in the fact that the eternal church will be diverse, and I will be amazed by my Lord's presence and feel out of place no more. But, for now, missional theology avails to the TCK the hope of the things to come.

Another way missional theology helps the TCK is by helping show them that diversity not only is welcomed into the church but is near the core. The lynchpin of the gospel is that "Christ died for our sins." The secondary aspect is that the "our" is all who believe, "Jew first and the Greek." By understanding the great commission and the spread of the gospel (missional theology) a TCK can rest that they are included into the great heavenly multitude that John saw in Revelation 9.

Who Should I Listen To?

Missional theology focuses Timothy's mind to constantly remember the teachings of Jesus, and not the Judaizers. By teaching Timothy missional theology Paul helps Timothy not be distracted by cultural practices, but rather to be wholly focused on sharing the gospel to the world and rightly ministering to the redeemed. For the modern TCK, such a focus aids the TCK to not get bogged down with cultural differences in their church, but rather to focus on sharing the gospel. If biblical theology helps the TCK know their place in the kingdom, missional theology helps the TCK know their job in the kingdom. Yet, I believe personal evangelism is rarely practiced let alone espoused.

A further way that missional theology answers "who should I listen to?" is that it undermines the modern political messages by reminding us that the gospel is the salvation of man, not the salvation of ideals. As mentioned in prior chapters, TCKs are often pulled between political and cultural battles. In the church this often results in liberal versus conservative arguments, or capitalism versus socialism arguments, or social justice versus silent justice arguments. Missional theology confronts these polarizing topics with the truth that we, the church, are here on earth to spread the gospel of salvation, not the salvation of any ideal. While some may quote Mic. 6:8 in response, I'd remind you that the text reads, "To act justly and to love mercy and to walk humbly with your God." Missional theology holds the reality that God's mechanism of righting the wrongs of the world is within the church (those who walk with God), not outside of the church. As a mentor said, "if the world looks more holy than the church, then what is the point of the church? The church will always differ from society, for we 'walk humbly with our God.'" Thus, we can summarize Ephesians and the church as such, "the Father planned the church, the Son purchased the church, the Spirit empowers the church." Missional theology focuses the TCKs mind to the church, and not to geopolitical arguments.

How Does the Gospel Apply to Me?

Not only did the mission lead to Timothy's inclusion, but it also gave purpose for him in spreading the good news. As previously noted, missional theology not only helped Timothy to know how the gospel got to him, but it also helped him understand the gospel through him. Thus, the gospel applies because all are welcomed, and all are empowered by the gospel. For the TCK missional theology is the explanation for why the local church wants diversity. Missional theology also is the explanation for why the church should cry out for unity. Within these two explanations the TCK can find not only their place in the church, but also their purpose of helping diversify and unify the church!

Questions for Conversations

TCK:

- Have you been taught the concept of missions/evangelism?
- How does the concept of the gospel existing to be spread affect your thinking?

Minister/Parent and TCK:

- As a minister/parent, do you articulate the need/concept of missions?
- How can your church/family focus more on missions?
- What are the implications of not implementing missional theology?
- What key insight did you glean from this section? And how do you plan to integrate the insight into your life/ministry?

The third and final type of theology is table theology, or as we say in Spanish "Teologia de la mesa." First, by grasping the story of God, Timothy finds his place. Second, by grasping the missional theology, Timothy finds his purpose. Third, by grasping table theology, Timothy finds his method. We see this concept when Paul in 1 Timothy 4 continues the theological discipleship:

> [11]Command and teach these things. [12]Let no one despise you for your youth, but set the believers an example in speech, in conduct, in love, in faith, in purity. [13]Until I come, devote yourself to the public reading of Scripture, to exhortation, to teaching. [14]Do not neglect the gift you have, which was given you by prophecy when the council of elders laid their hands on you. [15]Practice these things, immerse yourself in them, so that all may see your progress. [16]Keep a close watch on yourself and on the teaching. Persist in this, for by so doing you will save both yourself and your hearers.

As previously noted, often minority congregations accomplish discipleship through life among each other. Here in 1 Timothy Paul encourages Timothy to be the example, though young and mixed. Paul's table theology is one of continual practice in front of others. The result of Paul's encouragement of a table theology is found in the statement, "for by doing so you will save both yourself and your hearers." In Timothy's own life table theology is what led him to Christ and encouraged him to continue. As previously mentioned, Timothy's foray into the Christian life came through his mother and grandmother teaching and demonstrating the gospel for him. So, Timothy instinctively knew that Paul's encouragement of table theology was consistent not only with Scripture but with what Timothy already understood.

Why Don't I Feel Comfortable at My Church?

Table theology moves the church beyond cultural traditions, and into the common place of sound doctrine. When church doesn't represent the TCK it is crucial for the discipler to live life with the disciple, so they can be the sounding board as the "anchor adult." As mentioned before, the TCK may seem to be more mature than others and need less discipleship, yet when one lives life with a TCK the milieu of issues come to the fore and can be handled appropriately.

The impact of table theology on the TCK's comfortability in church was crucial in my life. I have had several critical mentors who helped me to learn my place in the missio dei, via table theology: John Gibson, Landon Dowden, Ken Easley, and Tommy Harrison. These men were pastors, teachers, and most importantly daily friends. When I didn't feel at home in my church, these men would make me feel welcome, or would remind me that in glory, the kingdom is one of diversity.

Who Should I Listen To?

Table theology answers this question via the discipler (Paul) rightly saying "imitate me as I imitate Christ." When we discuss teologia de la mesa we are talking about not only dinner conversations, but also the concept of familial imitation. The discipler has the privilege and obligation of showing the TCK how to live out the Christian faith, versus the TCK only hearing about the Christian faith through the lens of their church culture. However, for table theology to be applied in the TCK discipleship relationship, two aspects are required.

First, if one is to be a model for the TCK you must realize that your modeling can only be of certain aspects. Unless you are literally of the same cultural/ethnic makeup, you as a discipler will not be able to relate to the TCK fully. In Paul's relationship with Timothy, he was able to speak to the Jewish nature of Timothy because of ethnic and cultural relation. Paul was also able to speak to the Greek side of Timothy because of cultural familiarity, for Paul was born in Tarsus. In my life I have always been mentored by older white pastors/professors. These men were able to relate to my white culture side and though they didn't have cultural familiarity as Paul did, my mentors were able to point me in the direction of other resources that could help me work through my minority issues. Wisely, my mentors never presumed to know or understand what I was going through. Instead they listened and did their best to sympathize with me in minority issues, and helped me to grow in my white cultural familiarity.

The second reminder for someone being a model in a discipleship relationship is that you must first grasp the gospel rightly. What I mean is that several aspects of the gospel must be grasped appropriately: gospel in private, gospel in public, and gospel in corporate worship.

As mentioned earlier, the gospel is not only about the salvation of the individual, but also the reconciliation of mankind.

How Does the Gospel Apply to Me?

Table theology levels the field of who can represent the gospel. When a TCK doesn't feel represented or at home in a church, table theology brings to the fore the concept of the mixed believer being not only welcome into the people of God, but also the example setter. The words of encouragement to Timothy (1 Cor. 11:1) echo such a sentiment. Paul's message to Timothy concerning being an example can be read as encouragement for Timothy to break the mold and to be the example of Christianity. Another biblical example of a minority being hailed as the example can be found in the Good Samaritan.

If the noted population and ecclesiastic trends persist, the application of Paul's TCK discipleship will become even more necessary! As will be discussed later, having someone to relate to ethnically/culturally is paramount to discipling minority believers. Though the recent outcry for minority leadership in the church and academy has been ignored, the development of "Timothy" may yield persons capable of answering the cry for diverse leaders in the future.[8] As a result, the TCK Timothy will be able to relate to majority and minorities thus, helping to bring unity within one church.

PAUL'S MESSAGE OF TABLE THEOLOGY

I have always read 1 Tim. 4:12–16 in light of the reality that Timothy was a TCK. While this passage has been commented on and taught as an application for any minister, I believe that this passage read in correct setting is a message best understood by the TCK who lives cross-culturally as Timothy did. As a result, not only was this passage good for Timothy but is wise encouragement for modern TCKs and their ministry.

> [12]Let no one despise you for your youth, but set the believers an example in speech, in conduct, in love, in faith, in purity. [13]Until I come, devote yourself to the public reading of Scripture, to exhortation, to teaching. [14]Do not neglect the gift you have, which was given you by prophecy when the council of elders laid their hands on you. [15]Practice these things, immerse yourself in them, so that all may see your progress. [16]Keep a close watch on yourself and on the teaching. Persist in this, for by so doing you will save both yourself and your hearers. (1 Tim. 4:12–16)

Let no one despise you for your youth.

The word νεότητος (youth) in this text is utilized to describe someone up to forty years old. To those outside of minority culture, the reality of forty years old being called a youth is incomprehensible. In every Spanish church and Asian church, I have served, those under forty were literally called the youth. As a minority, we often struggle to garner respect from other minorities, for minority thinking is one of elder community leadership, and not the younger generation. Maybe you felt the call to ministry at a younger age and have begun the work of the ministry (even lay leadership), but struggle within your minority relationships. I would encourage you to have your Paul (discipler) vouch for you. We see Paul submit such an advocation in 1 Cor. 16:10–11 when Paul says, "If Timothy comes, see that he has nothing to fear among you, for he is doing the work of the Lord just as I am; therefore let no one despise him." Though cultural dynamics can be difficult, and you may be looked down on, stand firm in your calling and trust in those who validate the call in your life! Minister in whatever way the Lord has equipped you.

An Example in Speech

As a mixed person we are often caught in the crossfire of many arguments and cultural wars. The New Testament has recorded many speeches garnered against another populace. In the gospels there is hurtful speech said between Jews and Samaritans. The first occasion we meet Timothy within the book of Acts (Acts 16), Luke recorded hurtful speech garnered toward Timothy's Greek nature. Likewise, in the life of the early church one would not have found seasoned speech between Greeks and Jews. Paul's encouragement in context is to not speak like these who are polarizing. Undoubtedly, Timothy was caught in these cultural situations. As a TCK there will be temptation to take sides in arguments that need no side taken. I, however, always advocate for defending sound doctrine. So, as a TCK remember that our speech is to always be graceful (Col. 4:6; cf. Luke 4:22) and careful (Eph. 4:29, 31; 5:4, 12). As a TCK you will be more sensitive to situations and speech, utilize this intuition the Lord has granted you to be a means of godly speech!

Example in Conduct

The Greek word ἀναστροφῇ is best understood as manner of life, conduct, or behavior. The previously mentioned verbal discord in the early church came with difficult behavior. Several instances of dividing conduct can be seen in the New Testament. (1) The Greek widows and orphans were not being cared for (Acts 6:1–7). (2) Peter and others seemed to be ashamed associating with the Greeks in Galatia (Gal. 2:11–13). (3) The power struggle in the Roman church after the Edict of Claudius was lifted (Acts 18:2). As a mixed person we have the opportunity and burden of being an example for more people than the average pastor. The instances where you can lead as an example will be incalculable. Rather than following trends of the polarizing camps, be one who leads in conduct. Remember, you literally represent numerous groups of people, therefore you have the ability to help be an example to many! So for the TCK remember that your conduct is to be one of meekness and wisdom (James 3:13), displaying holiness, reverence, and purpose (1 Pet. 1:15–19). Though we often feel like we need to fit in, do not behave as some do, but rather be an example to all believers!

Example in Love

The Greek word here for love is ἀγάπη. A simple perusal of social media will show you just how little love there is between many Christians, especially when it comes to ethnic issues. Mixed believers have the opportunity to be examples in these instances. I believe that the TCK has an easier time fulfilling the command "love your neighbor as yourself" for they probably in part represent the neighbor (Matt. 22:38–39). When given the opportunity, speak of it and exemplify it. Show love between God and fellow believers (Matt. 22:37; 1 Jn. 4:11) and show love all of mankind, including our enemies (Matt. 22:39; 5:44). Though some may say that a mixed marriage shouldn't happen, you are the creation of a beautiful union. Allow the love of your parents to be a mechanism to speak the love of God to others.

Example in Faith

Timothy undoubtedly had the opportunity to "soap box" for he was a disciple of Paul and had the ear of many. Yet, Paul's encouragement here rings true for us, do not lose focus, but rather stay fervent about the Christian faith. What does it mean to be a TCK and be an example in faith? When someone looks at me, as a TCK, I want them to one day say that Mario was someone who possessed a strong belief in Christ (Heb. 11:6) and displayed the character of dependability (Rev. 2:10). As we discussed before, there are many preconceived notions about many cultures and peoples. We as TCK believers have the obligation of helping correct these primarily through our lives, not just our words. Not sure who told me this quote, but it is indeed how I strive to be an example in faith. "Tell of the Gospel of Christ constantly, and when necessary use words!"

Example in Purity

Walking in two worlds requires a different kind of purity than most others have to strive for. While it is impossible to know what exactly Paul means by purity here, to a TCK reader of the text, I take it to be social/cultural purity. Even in cases where cultures have come together to worship, there are often things not received by the opposite culture because they perceive it to be "weird or not-culturally permissible." In Asian households, for instance, we take our shoes off by the front door. This is a sign of respect for the family who worked hard to own the house. If you were to refuse taking your shoes off, this would be a sign not only of disrespect, but you are now making their place "impure." Many more examples exist in every culture, so as a TCK lead in example showing those of the opposite culture how to maintain a respectable purity. Indeed, this text could be referring to moral purity, but I think that in a cross-cultural ministry situation there is much to be gleaned in this sort of a reading.

Devote Yourself to the Public Reading of Scripture

Moving from lifestyle exhortations Paul encourages Timothy to the public reading of scripture. Throughout the world there is a practice of publicly reading scripture. So, the encouragement here for all TCKs is to not take lightly the weight of scripture. I often tell parishioners that they would not have high blood pressure if they read their Bibles as much as they watch the news. We as TCKs will be constantly pulled between worlds, ideals, methods, and places. Find your center in God's word! And when given the opportunity speak it aloud to others.

Devote to Exhortation and Teaching

Not every believer has the spiritual gift of exhortation and teaching. But every believer has the obligation to read the Word, and memorize the Word. I am often asked to speak on panels about racial topics, or even casually asked what I think about social situations. If I were not in the Word and memorizing the Word then I would articulate my personal ideals. As TCKs our objective is to unify the divided church and to share the glorious aspect of biblical unity, so quote scripture. I recall Dr. Olford once saying, "if you're going to say something that is contentious or difficult to accept, quote someone else!" Here I find that Paul's exhortation to Timothy is not only the encouragement of the liturgical norm, but also the encouragement to let scripture speak to issues, for then the naysayers will be taking fault with the God of the Text, not the messenger.

Do Not Neglect the Gift You Have

The last encouragement of Paul I want to apply to all believers. Though the text reads, the gift given by the laying on of hands, I propose the text can be understood as, "don't neglect the gifts given to you in your personhood and by the power of the Holy Spirit." You as an individual were not a surprise to God. You as a mixed individual were beautifully and wonderfully made. With your creation as a mixed believer you have wonderful opportunities and capabilities that others don't. So use them to God's glory. Rise up and speak on behalf of others, be the go-between cultures. Learn to live in the middle place for the sake of the kingdom. Why? As Paul said,

> [15]Practice these things, immerse yourself in them, so that all may see your progress. [16]Keep a close watch on yourself and on the teaching. Persist in this, for by so doing you will save both yourself and your hearers.

I do not believe Paul was advocating for justification salvation through Timothy's life, but rather I believe he was articulating that through Timothy's life believers may know the gospel rightly, and the whole body of Christ lovingly.

Questions for Conversations

TCK:

- Has anyone taken the time to explain to you how to live out the things you've heard preached at church?
- Of the points from 1 Tim. 4:12, which one resonates with you and why?
- Which of the points from 1 Tim. 4:12 do you wish that you could do better?

Minister/Parent and TCK:

- As a minister/parent, do you spend frequent time with parishioners explaining the things of God and the church to them in their lives?
- Have you ever considered 1 Tim. 4:12 in light of Timothy being a TCK?
- Of Paul's encouragements in 1 Tim. 4:12, which one do you think your church needs most from the TCK?
- What are the implications of not implementing table theology?
- What key insight did you glean from this section? And how do you plan to integrate the insight into your life/ministry?

TC IN SERVICE

When a church has TCKs or desires to, there must be a cultural shift in church leadership, style, and culture. However, to appropriately "make space for the TCK" one must confront our church's stance toward people of another ethnicity. The below are four "stages" or "stances" on other ethnicities.

View 1: Distance
  Attitude: "We do things separately."
  Viewpoint: They are different.
  Practice:
    We do things differently and separately.
    We don't understand them.
    We don't try to blend together.

Example: English Speaking Mission church of another ethnicity.

Impact on the TCK: The distance stance is the most detrimental to the TCK in your church, and sadly the most common church stance. When a TCK encounters a distance style church they will feel unwanted, misunderstood, and ostracized. If they do attend a distance style church, they run the risk of adopting these views into their ecclesiology and as a result have little in common with believers of another ethnicity. While the TCK believer may look like the minority mission church, they often do not culturally fit in as well as they do with the white church due to being raised in the United States. In New Orleans we have seen thousands of young believers caught in this quandary end up walking away from the church.

View 2: Respect
  Attitude: "We do things for them."
  Viewpoint: They are needy.
  Practice:
    We gather information about them.
    We intentionally seek to include them.
    We develop ways to help them.

Examples: Church with ethnic populous, who aren't represented in style.

Impact on the TCK: The respect stance brings more openness to the TCK but teaches a lie of cultural superiority. If a church adopts and applies the respect stance, they run the risk of castigating or constantly putting down the minority as someone who is always needy. The result of this put down is the subconscious lie being taught that minorities do not have anything to contribute! I have seen scores of good hermeneutical insights ignored just because it was coming from a "less educated minority." While the respect stance brings some ethnic relationships, these relationships seem to always be one sided, and the minorities and TCKs within this church will not remain for long.

View 3: Tolerance
  Attitude: "We let them do things with us."
  Viewpoint: They are acceptable.
  Practice:
    We invite them to join us.
    We practice our cultural distinctives.
    We hold the decision-making positions.

Examples: We let them show their specific ethnic style once in a while.

Impact on the TCK: Moving closer to an acceptable stance, the tolerance stance does not immediately hold cultural superiority like the respect stance but does whisper of it in the end. The TCK will find more comfort within the tolerance stance church. Here the TCK or their minority parent will be welcomed to participate in aspects of church. They may serve on worship team, teach a Sunday school, or even become a deacon. However, when one looks at the staff and elder board/church leadership council, only one ethnicity will be present. I've seen this reality in both white and brown churches. At first, I as a TCK felt at home, but when I realized that all the decision makers and staff are purposefully one ethnicity, I felt disrespected on one side or the other. A common phrase that helps to identify this stance is, "I / we don't see a reason to purposefully hire a minority." Or "It is prejudice to hire a minority over a white person" (more on these phrases later).

View 4: Love
  Attitude: "We do things with them."
  Viewpoint: They are equals.
  Practice:
    They have a role making decisions.
    They are represented in key leadership positions.
    Their cultural distinctives are utilized and supported.

Examples: Every ethnicity is represented in all levels of leadership, and style of the church.

Impact on the TCK: The love stance is where all churches should strive to be! The reality of shared leadership, cultural identity, and unique style respect is an earthly picture of John's revelation of heaven. I have only ever personally seen one church fulfill this picture, fellowship Memphis under the leadership of Bryan Loritts. I however want to be brutally honest; the love stance is the messiest of styles and requires submission from all parties participating. It is much easier to adopt any of the other stances than it is to fulfill this one. However, if you desire to reach TCKs and their parents (minority or majority) you must strive to make the love stance a reality in your church.

In 2005 I went with a mission group to Russia. I recall that on this trip only I and my friend Brandt were the only brown people on the team. We were not offended by this reality, for other minority students could not afford the trip, and we were friends with those on the trip with us. I remember the day we arrived in Moscow Brandt and I immediately noticed we were the only brown people in the airport! A day later, we realized this again, but in a Mosco mall. Awkwardly we noticed the reality when we visited a university and then at an orphanage. The result however at the orphanage was that the kids ran up to us, and feverishly rubbed our skin as though they wanted to help us wipe dirt off. Our translator told us, you guys are the first nonwhite people these kids have ever seen. Soon Brandt and I began feeling extremely home sick. Wisely our leader (my high school swim coach) told us to get in the van with her and the translator. We drove over to the nearest McDonalds in Moscow. There we ate our fill of big mac, fries, and shakes. Suddenly our home sickness dissipated and we felt as though we could make it the rest of the week. I now realize, our leader was giving us a taste of home to help us feel comfortable in a vastly different world. In church, the smallest of cultural tastes can help the TCK and mono-ethnic feel at home, though in a vastly different world. I encourage you to remember the love stance is a means of not only welcoming someone, but helping them feel welcomed.

Questions for Conversations

TCK:

- Which of the three theology types do you best relate to?
- Have you ever related your life to the full story of God? (missio dei)
- Which of the three do you wish your minister would articulate more to you?

Minister/Parent and TCK:

- As a minister were you trained to think/practice these three types of theology (even if named differently?)
- Which theology does your church most lack?
- What are the implications of not implementing all three of these theologies?
- What key insight did you glean from this section? And how do you plan to integrate the insight into your life/ministry?

CULTURAL SENSITIVITY

In the process of ministering to a TCK one must grasp the varying views of church culture. While your mind may immediately drift to music, clothing, and preaching styles, I encourage you to think about cultural purpose views. The aforementioned things may indeed be the most visible, but these aspects are often tied directly to cultural purposes of church. I don't intend for the following to be a label of any one particular ethnicity, for I have seen these represented in varying church contexts.

As you consider the following views, I'd recommend that you ask God to break you from the thinking that any one ethnicity is 100 percent correct! Ask God to give you eyes to see how others view the world. Ask God to break you of habits that are offensive to others.

God Experience

This view considers church to be their time to experience God. This is a high view of feeling and a low view of learning. Churches like this have a "freer" worship service that lasts for hours until they feel that the service is over. They may also change formality of the service so that the experience may be better achieved.

"And awe came upon every soul, and many wonders and signs were being done through the apostles . . . praising God and having favor with all the people. And the Lord added to their number day by day those who were being saved" (Acts 2:43). Many of our brethren desperately seek to get an experience. This is not different from the New Testament, except in the New Testament the God experience was brought about by the gospel, then worship followed. When we worship the Lord through the Word, we can't help but worship the Lord through song, dance, art, prayer, or whatever means you experience God through. If you don't relate to those who attend church for a God experience please do not look down upon those who want a God experience on Sunday morning. Maybe this is what C. S. Lewis was referring to? "The perfect church service would be one we were almost unaware of. Our attention would have been on God" (C. S. Lewis).

Duty

This view considers church to be a "duty" or "thing we do on Sundays." This view will leave the believer to feeling obligated to attend, and leave as soon as possible, and attend only when required.

Some would think immediately that this is a ridiculous view of church, but honestly it is also right. Hebrews 10:24–25: "Let us hold fast the confession of our hope without wavering, for he who promised is faithful. And let us consider how to stir up one another to love and good works, not neglecting to meet together, as is the habit of some, but encouraging one another, and all the more as you see the Day drawing near." If for no other reason you begin to be involved in a church, Heb. 10:25 is a beautiful example of a "God Said So Law." Differently than our friends who hold the "duty" view, scriptures paints the picture that it is our duty to be a part of the body of Christ. This doesn't just mean Sunday morning, but daily building one another up.

Learning

This view focuses away from worship/community and focuses primarily on the teaching time. God designed the church as a place where spiritual leaders could watch out for our welfare, as a shepherd guards the sheep. They watch out for you through teaching the Word. Hebrews 13:17: "Obey your leaders and submit to them, for they are keeping watch over your souls, as those who will have to give an account. Let them do this with joy and not with groaning, for that would be of no advantage to you." 1 Peter 5:1–3: "So I exhort the elders among you, . . . shepherd the flock of God that is among you, . . . but be an examples to the flock." Sadly many people don't know what good preaching and teaching is, therefore they look only for "meaningful worship." There is a needed twofold response. (1) Make sure that only those given the spiritual gift of preaching/teaching are doing the preaching and teaching. (2) If you are a preaching/teaching minded church body, do not neglect the opportunity to worship and rejoice in the Word for the day! Not responding to the Word is to not reply to a love letter.

Center of Community

Some ethnicities consider the church to be the central portion of the community. Often times this results in a longer day at the church, or much more time spent with the church as a family. Those who hold this view also often time get together as frequent as possible, much like a family.

As we consider the centrality of the church in our lives, we must remember if Christianity is "true then it must be of infinite importance. The only thing Christianity can't be is moderately important" (C. S. Lewis). Most of the time a church is visited as often as the gas station (only when we need more gas). Reality is that we're constantly on empty and in need of spiritual fuel. We get fuel not just from hearing the Word taught, but also from serving, receiving encouragement, and living out our spiritual responsibility. 1 Corinthians 12: We all have spiritual gifts and they aren't for your glory! 1 Peter 4:10: "As each has received a gift, use it to serve one another, as good stewards of God's varied grace."

- *We are to comfort one another (1 Thess. 4:18)*
- *Build up one another (1 Thess. 5:11)*
- *Confess our sins to one another (James 5:16)*
- *Pray for one another (James 5:16)*
- *Daily build one another up (Acts 2:42, Heb. 3:13)*

It is impossible to obey these directives if we only meet once or twice a week other believers. *If you don't like being involved and active then remember. "The church is not a dormitory for sleepers, it is an institution for workers; it is not a rest camp, it is a front line trench"* (Billy Sunday). If you only look to the church for community, I'd encourage you to remember that community is only possible because of Christ. Rejoice in the teaching, and rejoice in the worship.

In truth, all of the differing views of church are correct views. To live only in one of those views is to be one sided within the complex structure of what the gospel is to look like when lived out. In short, to live out only one of these views is to take an aspect of the church to excess, thus making the view wrong. Thus, a biblically diverse church is to reflect all the above attributes.

If you desire to reach the TCK and their mono-ethnic parents, you must keep in mind that your personal definition does not align with everyone's cultural difference. As shown earlier, the beauty of these varying ideals is that they are all biblical and can teach all of us an aspect of corporate worship.

So what do you do when you don't like someone else's view or difference of style?

- Pray—beg God to produce the true obedience and gospel in us.
- Pray on behalf of all ethnicities to receive understanding of differences.
- Meditate on the Cross (Eph. 4:32).
- Beg for a greater knowledge of the Word.
- Meditate on heaven that our relationships will be perfect.

It is a wonderful thing to diversify the view of church, but IT IS WRONG to force someone to divorce their cultural view of church. We must empathize with their view so that they can feel a sense of belonging. Otherwise, they will visit once and leave having no personal connection.

Questions for Conversations

TCK:

- Which of the three theology types do you best relate to?
- Have you ever related your life to the full story of God? (missio dei)
- Which of the three do you wish your minister would articulate more to you?

Minister/Parent and TCK:

- As a minister were you trained to think/practice these three types of theology (even if named differently?)
- Which theology does your church most lack?
- What are the implications of not implementing all three of these theologies?
- What key insight did you glean from this section? And how do you plan to integrate the insight into your life/ministry?

REPRESENTATION

When considering how to better minister to TCKs and people of mono-ethnicity in general the most pertinent and difficult topic is representation. This topic is where most take issue with my advice on multi-ethnicity and TCK ministry. I encourage you to consider the entirety of the representation topic through someone else's perspective as you read this section. I would further suggest asking a minority/TCK their opinion of this section.

Representation is pivotal to a minority believer. Personally, I analyze churches with three criteria. (1) Do they adhere to sound doctrine? (2) Do they have representation of minorities? (3) Do they have excellent preaching/teaching? Setting aside the doctrine and preaching aspects, representation is 30 percent the reason I will consider being a member at a church. I am willing to bet that representation is weighted even higher for mono-ethnic people. Why is this the case?

Reflect back to the prior discussion of Paul telling Timothy to imitate him. As stated, Timothy is able to imitate Paul in some respect, because Paul reflects half of Timothy's nature (his Jewish side). I suspect that Timothy may have agreed with my 30 percent weight of representation, for he is represented also by another ethnicity. For me, I do desire to see brown or white folks in a church (depending on the church), but it is not a deal breaker for me because I am half. However, those who are mono-ethnic will struggle to find some comfort in this type of a demographic. Such an imbalance of representation will yield the result of "tokenship." The believer will be the only ____ ethnicity and may withstand for a while but will quickly grow tired of being alone.

Before you think, "this is such an immature belief," I encourage you to try attending a church where you alone attend and are not represented in style, leadership, or population. I once encouraged a friend to do this, he came back to me in two months and said, "I can't take it any longer! I need to hear and see things familiar to me in church!" I laughed and he relented that there is indeed reason for representation. Why is this feeling the case in church where we are "one in Christ?" Simply put, Christians need mentors and models, not just pulpit fillers! While someone of a different ethnicity from you can indeed be a mentor or model, there will be so much lost in the cultural translation. As a young, brown, evangelical, reformed Baptist I have struggled to see or find minorities whom I can truly look to and strive to model my life and ministry after.

So how can a church best supply representation in such a diversifying world? I believe it is within the Timothy character that we find Greek and Jew best ministered to. The TCK has the unique ability to represent both sides. As I mentioned before, my college academic counselor encouraged me to check every box that applies for it is not only an asset to the school, but to me in reaching people. Likewise, the disciplers in churches must purposefully seek out the TCK, train them and empower them to help be an asset to the church! However, until TCKs are discipled and empowered to fill leadership roles we must admit the inherent awkwardness in tokenship and the cultural loneliness tokenship brings about.

In undergrad at Leavell College I took a course on church planting and revitalization. We had Ed Stetzer as a guest speaker one day. He said a phrase that has stuck with me, "what the people see is what the people will be." Thus, if you desire to be a diverse church, because the gospel encourages this reality, then you must diversify your stage. But, let's not confuse tokenship with true diversity.

> Confusing racial tokenism with progress provides some denominations and associations with a false sense of progress. To decorate agencies, committees, and staffs with racial minorities, as if they were ornaments on a Christmas tree, so as to give the appearance of progress, is unacceptable. These are tokens, people of color who are invited to strengthen existing systems and further the captivity of the dominant culture. There is a difference between being invited to sit on a committee as a token representative and being asked to lead the committee, staff, or agency.[9]

So, as we consider representation please don't think as shy as having a few minority members in pews being sufficient to bring about the comfort of representation to the TCK or minority parent. I do however understand that there will be a phase of tokenship until a populace is truly built up. Thus, when pursuing representation, you must have frank conversations with the first few handfuls of TCKs and minorities coming into your church, so that they know of the desired outcome. Furthermore, to expedite this awkward phase, I suggest quickly empowering the minorities so that visitors can see, though the number is low there is a place of prominence within the church for the different cultured! (There is more on this topic in chapter 4.)

Questions for Conversations

TCK:

- Who do you best relate to culturally speaking?
- How does it make you feel if you are the only or one of the few?
- Which position do you wish would be diversified first?

Minister/Parent and TCK:

- What is your church's diversity, in membership?
- What is your church's diversity, in leadership?
- Do you think that you are providing members enough leaders to relate to?
- What key insight did you glean from this section? And how do you plan to integrate the insight into your life/ministry?

LINGUISTIC DIVERSIFICATION

If you thought diversifying the views of church and the representation on the stage was difficult, just wait till you try linguistic diversification! Here's where the TCK becomes the unique go-between. When a church tries to become multi-ethnic there inevitably is a linguistic barrier developed. This barrier, however, is often with the first-generation immigrant parent. But, if you desire to adequately reach the TCK and empower them to be a go-between you must realize that there is a sense of fluidity in TCK language.

When I was the Hispanic youth intern at Dawson Memorial Baptist church in Birmingham, the youth spoke what is best termed Spanglish. Purposefully at lunch on Sundays they would alternate each sentence from English to Spanish. This game of linguistic hopscotch can truly help anyone grasp a language better. That was the reason, we did this game to help those with poor English or Spanish get better in the respective language. In church however, the youth only utilized Spanish. Another church which I served for a short time in Memphis was First International Baptist Church. In service we would sing songs in varying languages, but always had other languages projected on the screen. When it came time for Scripture reading each linguistic group designated a different member to read the passage in their respective language. When it came to peaching all preaching was in English.

For those of us raised in Christian households, worship music and scripture are intrinsically connected to a specific language. In essence, memories and the feeling of home can be brought about by linguistically diversifying the service. I personally prefer modern worship in Spanish and French, but hymns and scripture in English. So for me I'd prefer the service look more like First International than the monolinguistic Spanish or English church.

Linguistic diversification is not solely held to actual languages. When ministering to a TCK you must be cognizant of your word choices. As mentioned in earlier chapters, most TCKs will avoid polarizing terms and topics. The reason is because we often have a familial respect of both sides of the argument. I however know that most churches are adamite about certain geopolitical topics. However, most TCKs are "too liberal for their conservative friends and too conservative for their liberal friends." So, when a church pastor or any member of a church espouses polarizing beliefs the

TCK will most likely feel disrespect toward half of their family. Thus, if you want to minister to TCKs pursue neutral language, and help encourage such conversation in the church. Once again, I do not condone nor suggest leaving sound doctrine, thus the encouragement to Timothy to adhere to it! (1 Tim. 4:6; 2 Tim. 1:13).

Questions for Conversations

TCK:

- What is your linguistic preferences in church?
- If you could add one more language to your church which would it be?
- What topics make you most uncomfortable?

Minister/Parent and TCK:

- Does your church have diverse linguistics in service?
- What would the implications be if linguistic diversity were implemented?
- How can you help the church avoid polarizing topics?
- What are the implications of not implementing linguistic care?
- What key insight did you glean from this section? And how do you plan to integrate the insight into your life/ministry?

TIMOTHY PROTECTION

As a pastor/ minister you have the biblical obligation to protect your sheep. That being said, protecting a TCK requires different areas of protection than one may realize. In the example of Paul we see five major ways Paul protected Timothy. Within these five areas we can learn to protect and subsequently train TCK members.

Defend Diverse Practices

My second favorite New Testament book to translate and teach is Galatians. In this letter we see an interesting altercation between Paul and Peter (Gal. 2:11–14). Peter had been eating with the Gentiles and then Peter pulled away and acted hypocritically when the disciples of James came. The text is not explicitly clear as to why Peter pulled away, but maybe two things could be at play. (1) He was ashamed of eating non-kosher food. (2) He was ashamed of socializing with Greeks. Paul does not pull away from the table, but rather calls out Peter and the disciples of James for their behavior was, "not in step with the Gospel." Paul understood the gospel to transcend any prior dietary or friendship laws.

Defending the diverse practice of a TCK in church may mean defending their strange customs, food, Bible translation, or worship. Some cultures teach strict separation between the sexes within the church sanctuary, so the TCK who refuses to sit near a male/female may be accused of many things, when in truth they are practicing culturally correct worship separation. Some cultures fast every Sunday and need cultural sensitivity at potlucks. I remember the first time I met a half Burmese believer, we were at a church potluck Sunday and he sat alone without a cup or plate. So, I quickly ran over and offered to get whatever he wanted. He then educated me to the fasting practice and his silent ongoing prayer for the persecuted Burmese family, in Burma. The pastor and I spoke later and determined on Potluck Sundays we'd offer a room for prayer and scripture reading for those who practiced the weekly fast. While on the topic of food, sometimes the TCK may bring a very strange smelling/looking food to church potluck, I encourage you to be first in line to try it! The acceptance of a leader in the church sets a strong example for all members watching.

The list of alien practices has no end. As a minister of a TCK, you must see these practices, acknowledge their reasoning, help accommodate when needed, and then help educate other inquisitive members. By no means will I ever say that you as a minister must defend, accommodate, and teach others bad theology/doctrine held by a TCK. Remember what Paul encourages Titus, "Teach what accords with sound doctrine" (Titus 2:1).

Defend Diverse Interpretation

Though bad theology is not to be espoused and defended, diverse interpretations should be! When one grows up in a minority church you hear numerous interpretations of passages, which differ from majority-culture preaching. I have attended five theological institutions, and hold a PhD in biblical interpretation, but was never told to read a minority scholar or a minority interpretation text.

I was surprised when a professor presented a Greek exegesis on the Good Samaritan. I and numerous minority scholars in the room pushed back via asking if he had consulted or read any minority scholars of the passage, such as Martin Luther King Jr. The professor's reply was that he had not. I do not believe that Dr. Price blatantly disregarded minority hermeneutics, but he clearly was not brought up hearing the passage read as a minority preacher reads it.

Thus when ministering to a TCK you must be aware of the vast array of interpretations of passages, for the TCK may be raised to understand the passage in one light, and a contrasting interpretation could become detrimental to their spiritual walk if presented wrongly. The means of defending diverse interpretations is to be broadly read, culturally competent, and doctrinally grounded. Most minority interpretations of passages are unique because they are geared toward the minority context. Some however do handle the passage incorrectly, thus the need for doctrinal grounding, so as to prevent bad theology.

Anti-Political

I often say that the fastest way to diversify a church is music and the fastest way to split a church is to talk about politics. I know that politics is intrinsically connected to the pulpit in some churches. However, these churches rarely have a diverse congregation. Thus, if you desire to minister to the TCK do not talk about politics from the pulpit, but do preach biblical standards!

As a TCK if someone begins preaching about why the congregation should vote for X candidate or X party, I immediately tune them out. Instead when it is voting year/season I appreciate a pastor who comes to the season and rightly reminds believers of biblical standards, both in moral areas and in character. Sadly, many believers fall prey to a singular political party and as a result, overlook biblical morals and ethics. Yet as a TCK we are often stuck between the two worlds thus a reminder of scriptural norms helps paint a place for the TCK to belong.

Share in Leadership

Another way that we see Paul defend Timothy is by giving him a role. When doubters of Timothy pointed to his Greek heritage, Paul undermined their argument by empowering Timothy. What a better way to defend someone than to give your approval of them via empowering them to a leadership position.

I recall one church I served in Memphis had a single black member. This man was not only black but had special needs. He however was high functioning and desired to be part of that church despite the looks and snide remarks. The older worship pastor of the church, in one leadership meeting, voted that we empower this man to be an usher and leader of the greeting team. While we knew that he would need much help in the leadership role, we knew that this would aid in defending him against the naysayers. Indeed, within two months, all doubts, looks, and remarks were gone. Sadly, I found out that the church secretary continued to harbor prejudice views of not only this man but also me.

Each church has a place where a TCK can be empowered. Most churches have teams such as greeting, ushers, food station, media, scripture readers, worship teams, the choir, and many more. These teams can show others the value of a minority within the church.

Welcome Him into Places Not Typically Shared

Where the previously mentioned teams are a good way of defending Timothy, welcoming Timothy into places not typically shared empowers Timothy and further defends him. Places that are not commonly shared are sanctuaries, pastoral meetings, study/prep for preaching, service de-briefings, and onstage leadership.

I recall working for one church where they actively practiced the distance stance with another ethnic populace (Ethiopian). When a new associate pastor came in, he decided this had to change but the members were uncomfortable with the minority populace. They were okay letting them utilize the gym, but not the sanctuary, or even regular classrooms. Thus, the pastor decided to help the members break their prejudice, he would let the minority ministry meet in the sanctuary while the white majority had Sunday school, and then they'd use the Sunday school rooms while the English congregation met in the sanctuary. The result of this was during the between times, both populaces had to share hallways, bathrooms, and parking lots. Within one year there was crossover between services. Minorities were trying their best to learn English in the English service and the English members were trying their best to learn Amharic in the minority service. More beautiful than the service crossover was the unification of the children's and youth ministries. The kids and teens already attended school together, so this unification was only natural and will result in a truly multi-ethnic church of the future.

When minorities are welcomed into places not typically shared, like in the abovementioned occasion, TCKs will find a place to be comfortable. Churches that have such crossover do a much better job of reaching the second and third generation immigrant than the typical distance stance church does.

Questions for Conversations

TCK:

- Which of the three theology types do you best relate to?
- Have you ever related your life to the full story of God? (missio dei)
- Which of the three do you wish your minister would articulate more to you?

Minister/Parent and TCK:

- As a minister were you trained to think/practice these three types of theology (even if named differently?)
- Which theology does your church most lack?
- What are the implications of not implementing all three of these theologies?

- What key insight did you glean from this section? And how do you plan to integrate the insight into your life/ministry?

TC IN PREACHING

Within multi-ethnic ministry and ministry to TCKs there are two main ministries to carefully modify: preaching and worship. I would say both are just as equally weighted, thus this section and the worship ministry section could be alternated. What is clear is that if you modify one, you should modify the other, otherwise it will seem that your pastor or worship team are "not on board" with diverse ministry. Regarding preaching there are three ways to adjust your preaching to care for the TCK: illustrations, cultural sensitivity, and political avoidance.

Cultural Sensitivity

A preacher keenly aware of TCKs and minorities in his congregation will be culturally sensitive. Preaching in a culturally sensitive way requires knowing the culture of the people in the audience. Far too often preachers are strictly that ____ preachers. If you desire to be one who properly preaches across ethnic lines, you must pastor! Like a shepherd, live among the sheep, know them, know their likes and dislikes, then feed according to this. A culturally insensitive preacher is one who blatantly ignores culturally sensitive topics, or purposefully throws them in the face of the hearers.

I had a friend who, every chance he got, preached against the Republican Party. I confronted him because the churches he was consistently invited to were small rural white churches who were almost 100 percent Republican. If he were culturally sensitive, he would not have brought up politics, nor would he have purposefully chosen to confront churches on views which they nearly 100 percent held to. Another preacher I once heard utilized a lot of World War II illustrations and constantly berated the Germans. If he had culturally been aware, he might have realized that nearly 40 percent of the church members were German immigrants, many of whom had previous generations die in the war.

The main way to be culturally sensitive is to live among the people. However, if you are a guest speaker I encourage you to utilize a vast array of word choices and cultural illustrations so as to speak to any that are present. In the life of a TCK preacher, we can accomplish this via talking about our family's lives and dynamics. The diversity within our makeup often yields a point for most to connect to.

Illustrations

There are two schools of thought when it comes to illustrations. One school says that the preacher must research and scour the world for the best illustration for the sermon, the upcoming Sunday. The other school of thought says focus on the Word and let the illustration flow out of the overflow of knowing your people and you knowing the text. I was trained by preachers of the second school of thought. As a result, I spend very little time researching or looking for illustrations, but I spend loads of time listening and thinking about my people.

If you desire to preach a sermon which reaches the TCK or people of another ethnicity for that matter, you must know them and their culture. Then and only then can you begin a search for the "perfect illustration." If you do not know your people, you could utilize the wrong reference when trying to speak through their cultural lens. I recall a friend once spent a ton of time researching and preparing his sermon, utilizing Mexican history for illustrations. Sadly, he found out that the church he was invited to preach in, though Spanish, was full of Cubans. Let's just say the Hindenburg was a joke by comparison to how bad his illustrations went over.

So, as one who preaches often in varying contexts to varying ethnicities I'd like to offer a few ways to help you more carefully construct illustrations. (1) Know who is in the congregation. In the case of a TCK know what their diversity is. (2) Know how much they know/relate to their backgrounds. I had numerous German immigrant families in my New Orleans church, but none of them are culturally German, thus I did not research German illustrations. (3) When you research illustrations, do not pick illustrations that only reach one populace within the congregation. My training pastor Dr. Landon Dowden always encouraged us to "not bore the judge in the front row nor lose the attention of the 5 year old in the back." That of course is impossible, in my mind, yet it is what I constantly strive for. (4) Never let an illustration take away from the centrality of scripture and the message of the passage! In preaching class, we always love to discuss television preachers who are long winded in their illustrations, and nonexistent in the Bible reading. Never forget, the text is the word of God for the people of God. It is the reason you're in the pulpit and what the people need to grasp. Therefore, utilize the illustration to help convey the text and lead the hearer to desire to live out the text!

Political Avoidance

I have brought the topic of politics up before, but desire to flesh it out fully here. Sometimes I think that the most powerful and popular denominations in America aren't even churches. They are not the Baptists, Catholics, Methodists, or Assemblies of God. It's "political-denominations"—the Red versus Blue/Right versus Left argument. Do you doubt the power of political-denominations? Just try speaking against the majority within any church, you'll quickly see blood pressure rise, and people who wouldn't raise a hand in worship will begin pointing fingers faster than gunslingers in the O.K. Corral. In the movie *The Patriot*, there is a scene where Mel Gibson walks into an American pub and yells "God Save the King." He was quickly banished with a flurry of thrown food, knives, and gun shots. Though the articles being thrown probably won't be physical, you will be banished just as quick if you say a wrong political phrase.

Politics is a hot topic because all Americans are patriots whether you consider them to be or not. All Americans have a view when it comes to politics, even if it is an uninformed or an insensitive one. The Spanish church I was intern at in Birmingham had diverse political views. Those who "did it the right way" didn't like those who were "illegals." Even though this may have been the political stance, the pastor never discussed these politics. He always preached the Christian response to political topics. Members never quoted forefathers or the constitution, rather they quoted Jesus or Paul on a topic. Like I told one of the guys in my discipleship group, if we are people of the book, let our words always be seasoned with the "salt" of the Word. If our words are from the Word, then it won't matter what side of the isle we grew up on.

Keep in mind some biblical truths are not easy to swallow if you are from a different background. Learn to be sensitive toward other's views. In a diverse church you will encounter believers with different world views from yours. Just remember we're all a part of the same body and need each other. When it comes to political distinctives we must know all human views to relate to, and biblical views to correct with.

Preach the Text

The last and most obvious encouragement for those who wish to minister to a TCK is to preach the text.

> I once preached a sermon sheepishly apologizing for what the Scripture was saying. I then went home wept and vowed never again to apologize for God's Word. (Landon Dowden, PhD)

Many people are accustomed to hearing "feel good" topical sermons, which may invoke some change in the hearer's life, but this change is often temporary or false. When we consider how the preachers in the Bible handled the Word they recognized that it would be through Word that lives would be changed (see Gen. 1:3, Isa. 55:10–11, Acts 12:24). This means that if preachers want their sermons to be filled with God's power, they must preach what God says. God never says a one-line statement without implications that flow throughout the whole of scripture, therefore we must deliver sermons from all genres, testaments, and covenants.

By preaching the whole counsel of God we will handle difficult passages, which may convict us as preachers, but in turn will transform the lives of our congregation. In modern terms declaring the whole counsel of God is exegetical preaching. Levitical priests taught the law (Deut. 33:10), Ezra and the Levites read from the law and gave the sense of it (Neh. 8:8), and Peter and the apostles expounded scripture and urged their hearers to respond with repentance and faith (Acts 2:14–41, 13:16–47).

Exegesis is when a preacher takes the passage and expounds upon the main points and implications of the passage, even the culturally difficult passages. This pattern of preaching differs greatly from topical preaching, because topical sermons often rely upon a person's ability to superimpose topics over passages that may not handle that topic. So we know God condemns those who "speak of their own imagination, not from the mouth of the Lord" (Jer. 23:16, 18, 21–22).

Expositional preaching is important because God's Word is what convicts, converts, builds up, and sanctifies God's people (Heb. 4:12; 1 Pet. 1:23; 1 Thess. 2:13; John 17:17). Preaching that makes the main point of the text the main point of the sermon makes God's agenda rule the church, not the preacher's. The moment that a preacher relies upon his "amazing illustrations" and not the amazing Cross of Christ is the moment that the pastor will miss the gospel. Ephesians 4:13 calls every minister to grow all believers to maturity. Without preaching the whole counsel of God, we're leaving holes in every parishioner's life thus lacking understanding of the entirety of the gospel.

Questions for Conversations

TCK:

- What type of preaching do you best relate to?
- What is more important to you illustrations or handling of the biblical text?

Minister/Parent and TCK:

- Do you think about your audience when preparing a sermon?
- How do you prepare a sermon for people of a different ethnicity?

- How can a TCK help you grow in your delivery and preparation for other ethnicities?
- What key insight did you glean from this section? And how do you plan to integrate the insight into your life/ministry?

TC IN WORSHIP

I believe that there is nothing more personal in church than the musical aspect of worship. Dr. Martin Luther King Jr. wrote, "I was convinced that worship at its best is a social experience with people of all levels of life coming together to realize their oneness and unity under God." Dr. King was correct, when we worship our hearts are open to the Lord and we can see the heart of worship within our fellow believer.

If we were honest with ourselves, we have a musical preference for worship time in church. If you close your eyes and think of musical worship, you'll probably be lead to think about your favorite hymn, chorus, gospel song, or Latin praise. I believe if someone is striving to diversify a church ministry the greatest stumbling block will be musical preference. Musical style is the greatest way to determine what the ethnic composition of a church will be.

> There is no one-size-fits-all method or approach to multicultural worship. Each congregation and combination of cultures is unique. (Gerardo Marti)

We should be aware when selecting musical style and leadership that music affects every ethnicity in different ways. For mono-ethnic churches that are still fighting the worship war remember music affects not just ethnicities, but also every believer in unique ways. So, when it comes to worship be mindful of personal desires and needs with connecting. I'm not suggesting that you rid of your personal music preference. I am suggesting that you help your new brothers and sisters worship the Lord.

My wife and I chose a church based on a couple of criteria (preaching, diversity in the congregation). We did not pick according to music, but that doesn't mean that my heart doesn't desperately yearn for a Latin worship song. Every Sunday morning I can read the faces of believers around me; some older white believers, hurt because there isn't a hymn for them to relate to; black believers, hurt because there isn't a gospel song that reminds them of their childhood in church. You will even see younger believers who desire a "freer" worship song like Jesus Culture, or Hillsong.

Music should be like a good quality buffet. At Samford University (where I attended my freshman year of college) we had a four-star buffet in the cafeteria. No two days had exactly the same type of food. There was always pizza, salad, Italian, home cooking, and international. If you were to try to guess what was on each of those buffets, you probably couldn't guess it. Music is the same way in my mind. You don't always have to have two hymns, two choruses, two gospel choir pieces, and two Latin praise songs. Change it up just like a good buffet, but offer choices!

To have a successful buffet you need a well-trained cooking staff, with an excellent head chef. I recall once on the Italian buffet that lasagna was being offered, as was usual once a month. But it was more amazing than the last come to find out the chef that day specialized in Italian food in culinary school. I am speaking to myself as a worship pastor, we must know our limitations. If we try to "cook" something out of our specialty, it may be okay, but the people will know the difference between our lasagna and a true Italian chef's lasagna.

Be willing to trade days with another chef. At fellowship Memphis they had a rotating worship staff. I believe one of the interns told me they have four bands, and four worship leaders. The leaders and bands are just as diverse as the congregation. It was interesting to see how different populations really connected with different worship leaders and musical choices. Those few Sundays truly proved to me that diversity in worship is possible, beautiful, and pleasing to the father God. Keep in mind, no one style of worship was not represented every Sunday morning, so I am clearly not asking for you to divorce your worship preference, rather help your brother and sister in Christ worship through their heart worship.

Questions for Conversations

TCK:

- What music style do you best relate to?
- If you could make one musical change what would it be?

Minister/Parent and TCK:

- How can diversity in the music help equate to diversity in the pew?
- How can you help members slowly grow to appreciate various styles?
- What are the implications of not diversifying your church's worship?
- What key insight did you glean from this section? And how do you plan to integrate the insight into your life/ministry?

SUGGESTED READING

Crossover Preaching: Intercultural-Improvisational Homiletics in Conversation with Gardner C. Taylor by Jared E. Alcántara.
How to Share Christ with Your Friends of another Faith by Jeff Brawner.
Life Together by Dietrich Bonhoeffer.
For the City: Proclaiming and Living Out the Gospel by Matt Carter and Darrin Patrick
Multiply: Disciples Making Disciples by Francis Chan, Mark Beuving, and David Platt.
Multiethnic Conversations: An Eight-Week Journey toward Unity in Your Church by Mark DeYmaz.
Re:MIX: Transitioning Your Church to Living Color by Mark DeYmaz.
Ethnic Blends: Mixing Diversity into Your Local Church by Mark DeYmaz and Harry Li.
Holman Illustrated Guide to Biblical History: With Photos from the Archives of the Biblical Illustrator by Kendell H. Easley.
Third Culture Kids: A Gift to Care For by Ulrika Ernvik.
Growing Up: How to Be a Disciple Who Makes Disciples by Robby Gallaty.
Replicate: How to Create a Culture of Disciple-Making Right Where You Are by Robby Gallaty, Chris Swain, and Robert E. Coleman.
According to Plan: The Unfolding Revelation of God in the Bible by Graeme Goldworthy.
The Goldsworthy Trilogy by Graeme Goldworthy.
Discipleship That Fits: The Five Kinds of Relationships God Uses to Help Us Grow by Bobby Harrington, Alex Absalom, and Thom Rainer.
Intensional: Kingdom Ethnicity in a Divided World by D. A. Horton.
Christian Preaching and Worship in Multicultural Contexts: A Practical Theological Approach by Eunjoo Mary Kim and Mark R. Francis CSV.
Understanding Biblical Theology: A Comparison of Theory and Practice by Edward W. Klink, III, and Darian R. Lockett.
A Beginner's Guide to Crossing Cultures: Making Friends in a Multicultural World by Patty Lane.
Ministering Cross-Culturally: A Model for Effective Personal Relationships by Sherwood G. Lingenfelter and Marvin K. Mayers.
A Cross-Shaped Gospel: Reconciling Heaven and Earth by Bryan C. Loritts.
Insider Outsider: My Journey as a Stranger in White Evangelicalism and My Hope for Us All by Bryan C. Loritts.
Worship across the Racial Divide: Religious Music and the Multiracial Congregation by Gerardo Marti.
Intercultural Church: A Biblical Vision for an Age of Migration by Safwat Marzouk.
Raising Multiracial Children: Tools for Nurturing Identity in a Racialized World by Farzana Nayani, Velina Hasu Houston, and Paul Spickard.
Worship Outside The Music Box: Theology of Music & Worship and Multi-Ethnic Ministry by Stephen Michael Newby.

Let the Nations Be Glad!: The Supremacy Of God In Missions, 3rd edition, by John Piper.
Voices from the Margin: Interpreting the Bible in the Third World by R. S. Sugirtharajah.
Intercultural Theology, Volume Two: Theologies of Mission by Henning Wrogemann.
Worship across the Racial Divide: Religious Music and the Multiracial Congregation by Marti Gerardo.

Chapter 4

Your Pastor, the Third Culture Kid

During my time in Memphis, I worked for the Mid-South Baptist Association as an ethnic minority ministry intern. I and my partner Ken Lewis were tasked with determining the ethnographics of the community surrounding a church, and then help the church consider ways to better serve the surrounding ethnic community. As a result of this position, we both were stationed at several churches for short periods of time so as to help them consider and apply the research. During this job period, and ever since, many people have asked me how to move their church into being a multi-ethnic church. My response was then and still is today, "Hire a TCK/Timothy." Paul's statement in 1 Cor. 9:22 where he declared that he "became all things to all men, so as to reach some" is a natural state which we mixed people live in. Therefore, in this chapter I will discuss the reason for and preparation of a TCK to be a lead pastor.

EMPLOYING YOUR PASTOR

Between the years 2018 and 2020 New Orleans Baptist Theological Seminary, Southwestern Baptist Theological Seminary (SWBTS), Lifeway, the Louisiana Baptist Convention, the International Mission Board, the Southern Baptist Convention Executive Committee, and numerous other Southern Baptist presidencies were vacated. As reported by SBCVoices, a Southern Baptist news and opinion blog, the pool of presidential candidates were only white, with the exception of New Orleans Baptist Theological Seminary (NOBTS). The result of every presidential search was the hiring of a white president. A friend of mine posed a handful of interesting questions when this happened.

Why is it that "God's man" always looks like the majority? Are not some of our minority PhD friends men of God too? Are they not qualified since they have PhD's and leadership experience? Why didn't they get considered? Don't these search committees know how much it hurts to not see a minority in leadership? Don't these committees know how a minority leader can help change the SBC image? Don't they know how it can empower and change the dynamic of SBC ministry?

Undoubtedly my friend's questions and responses were a sentiment shared with others in the SBC. Hypothetically, what impact could have been seen if NOBTS were to have hired a black president in a city that is nearly 60 percent African American? What impact could that hire have had on the church in an era of national racial tension? What impact could have been seen if SWBTS were to have hired a Hispanic president in a region that is historically Spanish, but now is fraught with immigration tension? (Note: I believe that Drs Dew [NOBTS] and Greenway [SWBTS] are Godly, capable, and qualified men, who I pray for in their time of presidency.) The unfortunate reality is that any presidential search comes with politics. These SBC presidential searches are a national level picture of what often happens on the local church level, and my friend's questions are often on the mind of the minority parishioner.

In neighborhoods that have a mixed populace, or a shifting demographic, churches most of the time hire a pastor that looks like them. I am grateful that my church in New Orleans hired me, though the church was nearly 100 percent white. Interestingly, the pastor who preceded me was also Filipino. But, for churches that don't hire out of their demographic what is the reason? Do they not see the ministerial impact a minority pastor could afford their ministry? Why do many multi-ethnic churches that I know, who desire to be multi-ethnic in more than just their name, continue to only have white lead pastors? "While whites are the head ministers in more than two-thirds (70 percent) of multiracial congregations, the percentage of those led by black clergy has risen to 17 percent, up from fewer than 5 percent in 1998."[1] In my experience pastor search teams and presidential search committees are not operating from a place of racism. Rather, I believe there are numerous fears and subconscious reasons why churches, and institutions hire someone who looks like them. Not all of these reasons are found in each situation, but I have seen each reason in at least one situation.

Fear Cultural Change

The most obvious reason is that humans are creatures of habit and comfort. In other words, we like what we like. Therefore, naturally pastor search committees and presidential committees like candidates that are similar to their likes. In liking something that we like, we are by nature liking that which we already understand and can predict.

Have you ever been given a Pepsi when you were told it was Coke? I have and my mouth puckered, fingers curled, and I struggled not to spit it out. Why? Because when I see a brown fizzy drink and am told it is Coke, I expect it to taste a certain way. Likewise, when we are told someone is hired to be pastor, every Christian has expectations, regardless of ethnic background. Preaching, leadership, and ministry styles are often assumed, "why else would they be called to be our pastor?" But, when a pastor does them all in a culturally perceived contradictory way, you may have the same bodily response as I do to Pepsi.

If not done correctly, hiring someone outside of the cultural norm and style of the church can be detrimental to those who are not spiritually prepared for such a change. When helping one church consider how to diversify and reach the changing neighborhood, I suggested some staff additions (through equal eldership), not replacements. However, I later learned that the church pastor decided to step down so that the congregation would hire a black minister to replace him. The church made the selection and hire. Sadly, within six months most of the original families of the church left due to cultural differences. Three months after that, the church closed due to lack of funding.

I applaud churches that desire to make the cultural change, but I'd remind the elders, leaders, and ministers to minister to those that are among them, not just those that are outside of their congregation (1 Pet. 5:2). Though we may aspire to be a glimpse of the heavenly kingdom, we must not make such bold moves that the kingdom in our church remains divided, but now a different color.

Fear of Repercussions

I have applied to about 100 pastoral positions throughout the years. A common reply to my application is, "our people aren't ready for that." I laugh at such a reply because I do not think they've taken the time to investigate me, and my chameleon capabilities. However, they are articulating the unspoken truth that they fear repercussions for hiring a minority. I have heard numerous people hypothesize that few minorities are brought into presidencies because "the majority of financial SBC donors are old white folks." Whether or not this is true, the hypothesis further underlines the impact fear can have in the selection of a leader.

Fear Political Change

In the Deep South, most political lines fall fairly close to the ethnic lines. Though indeed there is some crossover, the majority however probably vote according to party lines. A fear within selecting a pastor different from the congregation is the fear of supporting X party and their ideology.

Juan Martinez offered a few simple questions to help think through political issues.[2]

- What is our vision of God's future? How do we envision the Rev. 7:9–10 worship scene? How does that vision impact how we do church today?
- What is our political vision of the United States? How is it impacted by our vision of the kingdom? And which informs which?
- Over the last few centuries, church and mission have often been tied to political and colonial power. Are we ready to break those molds?
- How do we deal with the sense of displacement that many majority-culture Christians will feel as minority groups become the majority in the United States?
- How do we break the patterns of racial identity politics that see others, particularly those from ethnic minority groups, as the "problem?"

I've been told, "We can't hire a Hispanic pastor, for we don't want to be viewed as the church which supports illegal immigration." I've also been told, "We don't want to hire a black pastor, because we don't want to support Democratic ideals of welfare and abortion." Sadly, in the Southern context, a pastor's skin color often comes with assumed political views. Lee Brand stated it well, "Don't be afraid that a person is going to go liberal just because they are a minority!"

With political ideology is often tied the "power" struggle. I've heard members say, "if we hire ___ ethnicity as our pastor, we're advocating for minorities to become the city leadership!" Some may say that such a power complex is at the heart of many institutional presidencies, for the majority does not want to lose power over whatever institution.

> Having an Asian, Latino, or black person sitting in a room, sitting on a committee, is different from ethnic members leading and determining future direction. This type of leadership transition requires whites to submit to the authority of nonwhites.[3]

As Lee Brand said, "don't be afraid that a minority candidate will go liberal." Worries about power shed light on the articulators' lack of trust in God's divine sovereignty. As one mentor constantly told me, "Jesus is either king over all, or he's king over nothing! That's how sovereignty works!"

They Only Know People Like Them

Another reason why churches and institutions hire people that look like them is that they associate with similar people. The pool from which churches hire is often a pool of known association. Such a hire is often the case with associate ministers who may be hired from within the city or church association. Thus, if your church is not connected with diverse associations then you will only have mono-ethnic pastoral recruits.

> When a position becomes available in most churches, leaders tend to contact those they know and trust, to inquire who they in turn might recommend for the job. The people we contact and those they recommend are, more often than not, people just like us in ethnic, economic, and educational background. Consequently, the people we know recommend people they know, and by the time decisions are made, the new hire—"the best person for the job"—looks like us as well.[4]

I know that within the SBC there are several minority groups that meet throughout the year, and at the yearly convention. However, churches looking for a diverse pastor rarely go into these groups and honestly ask for resumes. Likewise, I've heard numerous theological institutions saying that they want minority faculty, yet I rarely see a school representative enter the minority sections of the guild. Thus I advocate for not only going into these circles, but also knowing ones on hand. "Take minorities that are graduating from seminaries and get to know them! They are so much unclaimed talent being produced, yet not used!" (Lee Brand). You can only recruit those that you speak to!

Candidates Have Fears

Not only do churches have things to overcome when diversifying their pastorate, but many candidates have hindrances too! Like churches, candidates are accustomed to certain cultures and ideals. Thus, the idea of crossing a cultural line can bring about deep fear within the candidate. These fears may be right or wrong pending the situation. Though the candidate's fears can be suppressed, if they are not conquered, they will lead to a short tenure as pastor in a cross-cultural ministry. For the candidate to conquer the fear of crossing cultures they must grow in their understanding of the other culture and grow to be comfortable working within that culture. The last reason candidates have fears is the fear of being the token or first. Many pastoral candidates don't want to be the token hire. I have been the token brown minister in numerous churches, and it is a difficult place to minister from. It will be even more difficult for mono-cultured minority ministers, hence the candidates' fears.

Hire Timothy!

So once again, how can a church better cross-cultural/ethnic lines? Hire a TCK/Timothy. A TCK can help answer these noted issues in unique ways, just as Timothy was able to in the New Testament church. First the TCK conquers the fear of the different, because they are both different and yet familiar. Six studies have demonstrated that exposure to biracial individuals significantly reduces the endorsement of colorblindness.[5] I have found that though I am brown, I have been well received because I am also majority cultured. Once in a leadership role, I have been able to help introduce and move churches toward a healthier grasp of diversity, through my life and example in front of them. Second, the TCK is often easier to recruit than the mono-ethnic minority. When a pastor search committee, or other search committees begin their work, they will "fish" in the groups that they already indwell. The TCK as mentioned previously often resides in multiple groups, thus is probably already known to the committee. Last, the TCK most likely does not hold the same fears as the mono-cultured minority. We as TCKs already live crossing lines every day, and as a result constantly build cross-cultural relationships.[6] We're always the token ___ within a situation. As a result, we don't fear a particular culture, for we are accustomed to adapting to the situation we're placed within. So, if you want to move a church toward multi-ethnicity find a Timothy!

Questions for Conversations

TCK:

- Have you heard any fears listed earlier articulated within your church, when looking for new leadership?
- Of the noted candidate fears, which one do you most resonate with and why?

   Minister/Parent and TCK:

- What is the racial makeup of your church?
- What is the racial makeup of who you want your church to be?
- How would your church respond to hiring a minority leader?
- How might you better attract/recruit leaders of different backgrounds?
- What key insight did you glean from this section? And how do you plan to integrate the insight into your life/ministry?

THE POWER OF THE PULPIT AND A CASE FOR ELDERSHIP

When asked about diversifying pastoral staff, I typically talk about diversifying the pulpit, because the pulpit is the most important position to most churches! Why, because the preacher is viewed as the "place of power," or "the pastor." Indeed, you can make a dynamic change in a church by purposeful hires in numerous ministerial positions, but who you hire as the preacher will have the greatest impact. I have often heard minority reviews of a "white pastor, brown associate pastor" church as "white domineering." I know this is not the intention of the noted churches and I recognize that the review comes from a place of distrust. Nevertheless, let me encourage two ways to counter this issue; hire a TKC as preacher or have a diversified eldership that shares the pulpit.

Timothy in the Pulpit

One of the quickest ways to bring about trust from multiple ethnicities is to hire a TCK to be the preacher. If a congregation were to hire a multi-ethnic Timothy pastor, then they would be able to relate to multiple ethnicities and be the go-between multiple cultures. All of the research previously introduced in chapters 1 and 2 concerning TCKs can now become the reasons to hire a TCK as pastor. Most of the time, a TCK is ethnically diverse, culturally sensitive, culturally educated, linguistically sensitive, politically neutral, and situationally aware.

When the neighborhood changes, and the church desires to reach more than one ethnicity, a trained minister who personally represents multiple ethnicities can garner respect and trust from multiple sides much quicker than the mono-ethnic pastor. While the TCK pastor cannot be from every ethnic background, their diverse background can enable them the sensitivity and logic to operate in more cultures than the mono-ethnic pastor.

> On Sunday mornings people must see others that look like them or they will feel like outsiders. Whether intentionally or unintentionally unicultural, a church communicates nonverbally to other racial groups that they are the visitors and this is not "their" church. The goal, of course, is to make people feel welcome and accepted in our churches. In order for this to happen, we must be intentional about it.[7]

Another reason, as previously stated in chapter 3, to consider is that a pastor is more than a teacher, he/she is a mentor, model, and life leader. When the pulpit is only representative of one ethnicity/culture it is difficult for those in the congregation to learn from the preacher beyond the teaching in the pulpit. "When people identify others like themselves in our church, they know they are not alone and the church is indeed a place for them."[8] A TCK preacher can legitimately say to the congregation, "I am all things to all men so that I might reach some." The pastor can also say with greater ease, "imitate me as I imitate Christ." These reasons for the TCK in the pulpit are the reasons I believe Paul found, discipled, and empowered Timothy to the pastorate!

Share the Leadership

Another means of handling cultural/ethnic issues is to have a plurality of elders who share the pulpit. I believe a plurality of elders of various ethnicities will rid of power struggles. For my friends in traditional one pastor/senior pastor church polity, I believe it will be much harder to convey a picture of equality.

So why should we consider an elder polity? For those unfamiliar with eldership, this structure is similar to the often used "church council" approach, but elders are spiritually gifted and called men who pastor. Often deacons are put onto the elders list, but biblically I believe deacons are a different office. Depending upon your church tradition the leaders may be called bishop, elder, or pastor. My church roots are fundamental Baptist, but I have moved to attending and leading in Baptist churches which have a plurality of elders.

I advocate for eldership from the book of Numbers. In Numbers 11 we see the people desperate for food, so the Lord through Moses appoints seventy men to share in leadership, Spirit, and responsibility for feeding the people. This one instance is a great picture for New Testament Christians sharing the role in feeding the people (i.e., preaching). Through preaching the Word the elders lead the congregation as the Spirit leads in their personal lives. Elders are to be men filled with the Spirit and mature so that they do not take advantage of the congregation (1 Tim. 3:1–7 and Titus 1:5–9). So as to aid in protection, the plurality of elders offers accountability (Acts 14:23, Acts 20:17, 1 Tim. 4:14, 1 Tim. 5:17, James 5:14). I know firsthand how quickly an unchecked pastor can ruin a church and hundreds of lives. My first home church, an independent fundamental Baptist church, was torn apart by pastors gripped by sin and drunk on power. Thus, eldership can not only aid in showing diverse leadership, but prevent ministers from tearing up the church.

I can hear the voice of one of my mentors quoting the passage: "we are a holy nation a royal priesthood" (1 Pet. 2:5), therefore we all have leadership within the church. As funny as it may sound that is also true, but we are not all called to be the spiritual guides, shepherds, or "meat" providers. All believers are a holy priesthood who offer our own spiritual sacrifices (1 Pet. 2:5, Rom. 12:1). We are also all priests in that we have permission through the Spirit to enter "Boldly into the presence of God." Also, all believers are priests because we have all been gifted with varying gifts to help edify the whole body of Christ, beginning with our own household.

Each believer is given unique gifts for service to God. "We have different gifts, according to the grace given us" (Rom. 12:6). "Now to each one the manifestation of the Spirit is given for the common good" (1 Cor. 12:7). "But to each one of us grace has been given as Christ apportioned it" (Eph. 4:7). "Each one should use whatever gift he has received to serve others, faithfully administering God's grace in its various forms" (1 Pet. 4:10). As a result of these passages, we should understand the ministry of the church is not a one-man ministry.

Sadly, many people who yell for voting rights won't help in ministerial responsibility. I believe rightly teaching the concept of elders and their role of helping empower believers to do the work of the ministry will correct the broken norm of little cooperation. As quickly surveyed here, there are numerous reasons to advocate for eldership within a church, but for now, eldership offers a model which can help quell discomfort of all ethnicities, for the pulpit can be shared and still revered.

Questions for Conversations

TCK:

- In your respective cultures, how is the preacher viewed?
- Which culture preacher do you relate better to?

Minister/Parent and TCK:

- How have you viewed the preacher of a church?
- Do you understand the impact of the preacher over associate pastors?
- What implications are there if a church refuses to share the pulpit?
- What key insight did you glean from this section? And how do you plan to integrate the insight into your life/ministry?

TESTING TIMOTHY?

So, you have found a candidate to be your TCK Timothy and help develop a multi-ethnic church. Before hiring, you must determine if he/she is understanding, is called, and is gifted for this complicated task. Recently I've been heavily involved with testing and ordaining ministers. It has been a great blessing in my life that I am now someone to invite to these ordination functions. I am usually the one that shows up with several pages of questions (forty-seven to be exact). I think the purposeful hiring of a TCK requires unique deep questions. Here are a few questions to discuss with the TCK candidate.

What Do You Understand the Gospel to Be?

There are many ways that one can articulate the gospel, so don't look for a precise sentence or phrase. Here is the gospel, as noted in the introduction. God through Christ's death redeemed God's image thus correcting the sin problem begun in the Garden of Eden. In Christ's death he redeemed God's glory through bearing our sins, dying, and conquering the grave to attest that eternal life is available for all who believe (John 3). This may be where the majority of candidates stop. I'd encourage you to push and ask if there is more to the gospel in scripture? As Paul Harvey might say, "Here's the rest of the story." When God redeemed his glory through Christ's death, he reconciled man unto himself and as a result reconciled man to one another (1 Cor. 12, 2 Cor. 5). Thus, the second aspect of the gospel is the undoing of Babel, and the reunification of mankind (Acts 2). As a result, we see this unification of the nations pictured in the heavenly glory through John in Rev. 7:9. If your church or organization desires to diversify/better reach multiple ethnicities, it is crucial for the candidate to grasp both aspects of the gospel (God and man—and believer and believer).

In questioning pastoral candidates I've seen two primary answers. (1) They only articulate the reconciliation between God and man. I was raised in such a mentality, and as noted never heard the second aspect until meeting Bryan Loritts. (2) They grasp the first aspect, and tag onto it an earthly social justice message. This is indeed a loaded phrase, "earthy social justice message." But what I am advocating for is social justice among the people of God. We are reconciled together in Christ Jesus. Those outside of the gospel just won't get it! In fact, the argument for social justice, as portrayed in media, is a straw-man argument for the problem of injustice is a sin problem, not a political one! Only Christ can right this wrong through his salvation via the cross and through believers knowing victory over sin in their own hearts and lives.

What Is the Role of the Pastor?

Possibly my favorite question for pastoral candidates is always, "What is the role of the pastor?" Of course, in this question I am referring to any pastor, not just the preacher. Often however, candidates will answer, "to do the work of the ministry!" Let me push back and give a few biblical responses. First the pastor's job is not to do the work of the ministry alone, but to help equip the saints so that they can do the work of the ministry (Eph. 4:11). The ministry that pastors provide is to *feed* God's sheep God's word (John 21:15–17), *guide* the sheep (1 Tim. 4:16; 1 Pet. 5:3, Heb. 13:7), *protect* the sheep from attackers (Acts 20:27–29; 2 Tim. 4:3–4; Tit. 1:9), and *protect* themselves, and the church (Prov. 11:14; 24:6).

What Is Your Spiritual Calling?

I love Eph. 4:11 when Paul states, "And he gave the apostles, the prophets, the evangelists, the shepherds, and teacher, to equip the saints for the work of the ministry." It should be understood that all believers have a calling from the Lord which fulfills the "work of the ministry." Some of us are called to teach, preach, counsel, and so on, as seen in "typical ministries." Others are called to lawyer, business, firefight, police, and so on, as seen in what I call "lay ministries." What is clear from the text of Eph. 4:11 is that we are called to a specific ministry.

I do not approve of the historic blanket ordination for "the pastorate." I know that as Baptists, we have ordained men into "the Gospel ministry" for decades, and churches have suffered due to this. I have attended numerous churches where the ordained pastor was not gifted to be a pastor, and as a result the church closed. We should guide men and women to determine exactly how God has gifted and called them to accomplish the work of the ministry. Not everyone is a preacher, and not everyone is a counselor, but everyone has a specific calling. A person called of God should not take offense of this question, but rather take it to be liberating, for they can be honest about what they feel called to!

How Do You Know What Your Calling Is?

What if your TCK candidate doesn't know their specific calling? "With the billions of people on this planet, does it really matter that I do what God desires?" This question is like the myth that "my vote doesn't matter." If everyone were to show up and vote, then suddenly everyone's vote matters. But even if few people show up to vote, their vote really matters. Millions of Christians claim God's specific calling on their life doesn't matter, so those who listen to God's calling are even more important! For the sake of the gospel, listen to our Savior's call in your life! For he has called and will equip you for things you cannot even conceive of. My training pastor, Dr. Landon Dowden, told me a few great questions to help. I use these in every ordination council.

Have You Felt a Spiritual Urge to Do Something That You Are Not Naturally Gifted to Accomplish?

It may require great financial, emotional, and spiritual strength that you do not have on your own. Most of our heroes of the faith were not qualified to answer God's call, but through God's empowerment did. A true spiritual calling is one that requires complete reliance upon God.

Have Other People Suggested You Pursue a Particular Endeavor/Ministry?

I told someone at lunch today, often times other people see our giftedness and calling before we do. Parents do this with their little children, and friends do this with friends. A question I ask to ordination candidates is first who did you train under? Then, what ministerial areas did they suggest you pursue, and which ones did they suggest you refrain from? Friends may encourage you to a particular job, but others may hear you say your aspiration for a job and encourage you to change your mind. Listen to wise godly counsel. A great biblical example is the sending out of Paul. Saul (who was a religious zealot) meets the risen Christ on the road to Damascus, then is brought to the disciples who lay hands on him, and say that they believe God called/equipped him to bring the gospel to the gentiles. What a blessing that he had friends who did this, for nearly two-third of our New Testament comes from him doing this very ministry.

Have You Seen Results in This Ministry?

It is one thing to feel called, and hear friends encourage, it is another thing alltogether to have actual success in a particular ministry. (I define success here as personal faithfulness to the calling of God in your life and spiritual impact upon others.) I remember seeing and hearing many peers go through preaching courses and then walk away with a sense of a preaching call. Then, some in the class would encourage them by saying, "you're a good preacher you should preach." Years later, I find that these people are out of the ministry. What happened? They often respond, "I just wasn't good at it" (aka no results). Just because you learn the science of writing a sermon does not make one a gifted preacher. It is the same for any other area of ministry. I think this last step is crucial for pastoral candidates. If God has gifted you in a particular ministry you should see results from it.

How Does Being a TCK Inform Your Pastorate?

Without rewriting all of chapters 2 and 3 one should understand the diverse views that the TCK brings to the table when being considered as a candidate. They should be able to speak to diverse peoples and diverse situations and understand how to handle culturally difficult things. I would recommend asking them their life story and how it informs their view of the gospel. Then, ask how their view of the gospel informs their understanding of the pastorate. In these few questions you'll have countless hours of great conversation and be able to determine if the candidate is a good fit for your open position.

Questions for Conversations
TCK:

- Work through all the questions in this section.
- Which question gives you the greatest pause?
- Which questions would you add to these search team questions?

Minister/Parent and TCK:

- How does every search team candidate understand the gospel?
- Why is it important that the pastoral candidate understand the two aspects of the gospel?
- What if the pastoral candidate is not able to answer one of these questions? Which would you permit skipping and why?
- What key insight did you glean from this section? And how do you plan to integrate the insight into your life/ministry?

EMPOWERING YOUR PASTOR

So, you have found your TCK Timothy candidate, and you have questioned them. Now you've decided to move ahead with hiring. Having a TCK pastor requires several unique acts of care which are often overlooked in the life of a TCK pastor. Much like the discipleship relationship mentioned in chapter 3, your pastor requires lifelong care from the congregation and other ministers too. Here are five ways I wish that churches had empowered me as a TCK minister.

Empower Him by Reminding Him That He Is Wanted!

I have served approximately nine churches as a staff minister. Only at two churches was I told that I was wanted there, beyond the initial job offer. If you refer back to the psyche of the TCK, we struggle with the feeling of not belonging or being wanted. I have left churches because I felt undervalued, unwanted, overlooked, or even dismissed. If you purposefully hire a TCK to your ministry you must be aware of their inner battle of constantly feeling out of place and feeling that they don't belong. Help the TCK feel wanted by saying that they are wanted or by offering cards that articulate it.

Empower Him By Helping Him Stay Connected to His Cultures

When a TCK is hired to serve in a singular culture situation he/she will probably relate on many levels, but half of them will not relate. Reflecting back I would say my "perfect" pastoral position would be at a church that had white, Asian, and Hispanic cultures represented within the congregation. Then I could float between them and feel fully connected. But if your church does not have the TCKs respective cultures I'd encourage you to connect your pastor with ministries, ministers, or countries of their respective cultural need. One way that I have practiced such a cultural connection is to attend a different ethnic church when I can take a Sunday off. This little bit of difference is often all that I need to "hold me over" for the next little while. Your TCK pastor will probably yearn for different cultural aspects in church. Until those aspects are realized in your church, give him frequent freedom to visit another church so as to "recharge," and return focused on his pastorate.

Empower Him by Helping Him Stay Supported

The pastorate is a very lonely job. If your church has a plurality of elders or a larger pastoral staff, it can be less lonely. I remember moving from Memphis back to New Orleans to do my PhD and to be pastor of our little church. Though moving back home, these five years pastoring were extremely lonely! When a person takes on a pastorate, they also develop some strange separation from everyone else because, "you're pastor." Thus, developing close friends within the church is difficult.

TCKs, though culturally adept, suffer from loneliness more than your normal pastor. I and other TCK pastors often say, "I feel lonely in the thousand-person crowd." Help and support your pastor via helping him develop and find close friends. While fellow pastors can become friends, I have never developed those friendships because I don't want my close friends to talk about work all the time. I want close friends to talk about anything else!

Empower Him by Helping Him Grow

It is crucial to help your TCK pastor, or any pastor for that matter, to continue growing in knowledge. The following three areas should be considered: (1) TCK (2) ministerial, and (3) cultural.

If you are hiring a TCK minister I hope this work is a book that you will pass along to them. As mentioned, I did not truly understand myself until I became aware of TCK studies and saw that much of what I dealt with is a common side effect of being third cultured. Also, I hope that this book can serve as a launching point for your TCK pastor to read other books geared toward TCKs and TCK ministry.

Second, I wish that ministers had to get Continuing Education Unit (CEU's) just like other job fields. My wife, as a social worker, is required to accrue CEU's to maintain her social work license. These continued training hours are often new techniques, new laws, and review of already learned data. I would encourage any pastor, TCK or not, to continue recovering learned data, and to also grow in new things. Numerous seminaries and Bible schools offer continuing education classes for pastors. These often fall during summer, or winter breaks. In the realm of ministry, I would encourage the TCK to read cross-cultural texts and attend multi-ethnic ministry conferences to bolster the suggested reading.

The third area to encourage your TCK to grow is in cultural knowledge. Many different agencies will require their staff to go through "cultural education" before being permitted to begin their jobs. We see this with government officials who are working in another country on behalf of the United States, and many other multinational companies do the same thing.

Like Paul with Timothy, a church can encourage the TCK pastor to grow in their cultural knowledge. While a TCK has multiple ethnicities and cultures within themselves, there is always room for growth. This type of education will help them make fewer missteps and feel less awkward when engaging people across racial and cultural gaps. Cultural growth can come from building relationships with those in 100 percent of the culture, and from reading materials. Beyond these relationships here's a few bullet points to become more culturally sensitive:

1. Pray:
   Ask God to conform you to being sensitive to other's ethnic needs.
   Ask God to break down any prejudices that you may hold. (Trust Me! I the ethnic guy, even have prejudices that I've had to deal with.)
   Ask God to break you from the thinking that any one ethnicity is 100 percent correct!
   Ask God to give you eyes to see how others view the world.
   Ask God to break you of habits that are offensive to others.
2. Live among the people:
   Eat where they eat.
   Shop where they shop.
   Read what they read
   Watch what they watch.
   Play (if you have kids) where they play.
   Live (if you can move) where they live!
3. Befriend the people:
   Living among the people isn't enough!!!
   Build a genuine friendship with numerous ethnicities!
   Once a level of trust has been achieved ask the pertinent questions. (If you can have this conversation with several ethnicities at once, you will truly see the diversity in answers.)

Empower Him by Helping Him Know It Is Okay to Move, Should the Lord Lead

A final interesting way to empower a TCK culture comes from Paul and Timothy's relationship. Paul frequently sends Timothy from church to church. We can take from Paul's assigning Timothy to move to various churches that you can empower your TCK pastor by helping them know it is okay to move, should the Lord lead. In serving numerous churches throughout my ministerial career, one of the best graces shown to me was churches encouraging me to move to a new ministry where my help was needed more. In truth, there are fewer TCKs in ministry than mono-ethnic ministers. As a result, a TCK must be willing and flexible to move when they feel called to a new location. The church can empower Gods work in and through the TCK pastor's life by helping send him out much like Paul sent out Timothy.

Questions for Conversations

TCK:

- If you are a minister, which of the abovementioned ways of empowerment do you most need in your life?
- Which of the empowerment ideas have you experienced in your life?
- What other ways can a church empower their pastor?

Minister/Parent and TCK:

- How these levels of empowerment relate to any care of a pastor?
- Which level of empowerment is the most difficult to do for your pastor?
- How can a church better prepare to empower a minister to move ministries?
- What key insight did you glean from this section? And how do you plan to integrate the insight into your life/ministry?

TRAINING YOUR PASTOR: NOTES FOR SEMINARIES AND MINISTRY SCHOOLS

When considering how you can help train a TCK to be pastor I cannot understate how impactful a good quality seminary education, including mentorship, is. I was one that originally said I didn't need or want to attend seminary. Through the encouragement of numerous pastors, family members, and professors I went to seminary. In my experience, seminary is a completely different level of discipleship for those who desire to enter ministry. I do understand that not every seminary is the same, but very little compared to a quality seminary training.

I have attended five different theological institutions in my academic career. Only one of these institutions had a single minority on faculty. Furthermore, none of these institutions were tailoring any aspect to better help train minority or TCK students to better minister to minorities or minister in cross-cultural ministries. Thus, in hopes of helping seminaries and ministry schools better train TCKs like me, I would like to make some suggestions.

What Is a Minority?

I remember like it was yesterday. I was attending a meeting on intentional diversity. I and several other Hispanic and Asian attenders asked numerous questions about professors, books, and ministry training ideals. After the meeting I was speaking with one of the panelists when a significant leader in our local Baptist association butted in and stated, "well, in our city Black is what everyone means when they say 'minority.'" I asked him if he knew the history of Filipino, Vietnamese, and Cuban immigration to the city. He looked at me with surprise and said no. I responded, "Well sir, Filipinos have been here since 1780 when they were slaves on Spaniard ships and escaped. We have and always will be an integral minority here."

Knowing who surrounds your institution should inform your institution's strategic hiring and training programs. Not all minority groups are easily recognizable. In South Louisiana, we have a large contingency of deaf people. My mother has served the deaf community through interpreting and ministry my entire life. Throughout the United States deaf people exist and are a unique minority group within numerous ethnic groups. The deaf, according to all reports, are the least evangelized populace within the WORLD! Yet, to my knowledge, no seminary is offering a training program for deaf ministers to become deaf pastors. This reality has left the deaf pastorate for those who are hearing, or those who were trained by their pastor. If the association leader's statement were to be taken to heart, then the millions of deaf people will never know the gospel for no one is purposefully training pastors to reach these people.

My mother once told me how the Wizard of Oz, in black and white, was horrifying and scary. However, when she later saw the movie in color, she rather enjoyed it. Sadly, like my mother, I am horrified and scared because many schools are stuck in a two-color rhetoric. I hope that institutions who desire to minister minorities will realize that there are a slew of ethnicities in our world who need someone who can show them what it means to be X ethnicity and a biblical scholar or pastor.

Questions for Conversations

TCK:

- As a minority, how do you classify someone as minority?
- Do members of your family relegate the term "minority" to one ethnicity?

Minister/Parent and TCK:

- Who are the minorities within your area of ministry?
- Did you discover a populace that you didn't realize was present?
- What is the smallest minority group represented?
- Which minority groups have ministries directed to them and which ones do not?
- What assumptions are tied to the term "minority"?
- What key insight did you glean from this section? And how do you plan to integrate the insight into your life/ministry?

WHY DIVERSIFY LEADERSHIP AND FACULTY

I believe there are five reasons for diversity within faculty and leadership.

1) Diversity will ensure that these schools will not become irrelevant.
    Soong-Chan Rah pointed out that because of the realities of Christianity and Evangelicalism in particular, Evangelicalism will become nearly extinct in the United States if there is not intentional change to reach minorities.[9] Rah's belief is based upon minority population and non-evangelical population growth within the United States. Interestingly, as of now, 60 percent of the world's Christian population resides in Africa, Asia, and Latin America. Thus, further bolstering Rah's concern for Evangelicalism is the statistic that if immigration and family trends continue, by 2050 white will no longer be the majority. As diversity grows in America, America becomes more global in concept. Thus, "In a global context, however, such Western and even Anglo-American perspectives may be neither translatable nor as portable across cultures as we might think."[10] This is not to say that white people or white culture will be gone, but rather the cultural tables will shift. So, how will the church and training institutions respond to such a change? This data shows there is a need to diversify faculty, diversify training methods, and diversify ministers in the local church.
2) Diverse faculty are better equipped to model what it means to be a minority and a pastor/scholar.

I have great respect for my professors throughout my academic career. However, due to their difference in culture they do not serve as adequate examples for minority students. Studies have shown that children develop a preference of teacher depending on whether they share a social group with that person.[11] At some point, many schools lost sight of the fact that they were training the next generation of ministers and began to think of themselves strictly as being the schools of academics. While indeed many academics came out of these schools, the majority of the students they train will be ministers. Thus, what the students need are not academics, but skilled ministers who can quote Paul and say, "imitate me as I imitate Christ." I can speak on behalf of my minority seminary friends, we would prefer to have a minority professor/mentor over a professor who has a publication list ten pages long. Having a mentor to empathize with a student is close to the heart of discipleship. Therefore, I encourage you to find scholars who are disciplers first and happen to be academics too.

3) Diversity will ensure that schools are not mono-cultured in ministerial ideals.

If you have spent any significant amount of time in a minority church, you will immediately notice how different the ministry is. Customs, culture, time sensitivity, purpose, and numerous other factors mentioned in chapters 2 and 3 come to play in ministry. Yet, these varying views of ministry were never taught at the schools I attended. Rather, I was required to read and was lectured concerning what I would call "White church culture." This knowledge has aided me in ministering in white churches but fell flat when I crossed into Asian and Spanish churches. Suddenly all the pastoral ministry classes did not fit. The service planning and organizing classes did not fit. The family counseling classes did not fit. I would encourage schools to offer diverse professors teaching these classes, or even co-teaching these courses so that students will be better apprised of how to minister in these various contexts. As a result, not only will minority students understand how to better minister in minority contexts, but majority students will be culturally/ministerially aware of how to minister cross-culturally too! "The percentage of multiracial congregations in the United States nearly doubled from 1998 to 2012, with about one in five American congregants attending a place of worship that is racially mixed, according to a Baylor University study."[12]

4) Diversity will ensure that schools are not mono-cultured in hermeneutics.

I previously mentioned the topic of minority hermeneutics, but this topic needs to be reiterated here in the context of diversifying a seminary. Though I hold a PhD in biblical interpretation, I was never once required or recommended to read a minority scholar's hermeneutic of scripture. I knew that I had grown up hearing different readings of scripture, yet my five schools never once mentioned any similar hermeneutic. You have but to read the writings of third world international believers or even the late Martin Luther King Jr. to hear different understandings of texts. While I say different understandings, I am not meaning heretical hermeneutics, but rather hermeneutics which are culturally sensitive. As Lee Brand said, "You have to know minority hermeneutics in the modern church. These ways are different, and not necessarily wrong!" Sadly, I know several schools that have minority scholars as faculty, but they rarely feel free to introduce a minority hermeneutic of a text. I encourage seminaries to not only hire minority faculty for previously mentioned reasons, but also to teach minority hermeneutics.

5) Diversity will show to the world how the power of the gospel can unify and empower diverse people groups into a focused group.

If we desire for churches to no longer be divided but rather effective at multi-ethnic ministry then what a better place to lay the foundation for such an ideal than in the schools that train ministers. As Bradley stated, "for those of us born after the Civil Rights Movement, the discussion is focused not so much on reconciling past oppression, pain, tensions, and grievances, as on moving forward-putting on display before a watching world how the Gospel creates the platform for racial solidarity (Gal. 3:28)."[13] Historically many seminaries were established for one ethnicity only. I do not know of any seminary with such an ongoing stance. Yet, many seminaries still remain segregated, especially in the faculty. As Brand said, "Theological liberalism [in minority communities] is the unpaid bills of conservative institutions who would not let minorities in." Thus, a diversification of leadership can help shed historical lines, doctrinal liberalism, and truly show the power of the gospel within a historically divided realm.

Finally, yes, most American accreditation bureaus are now requiring diversity, but as schools of scripture and ministry I would hope this reason need not be invoked. The previous are what I believe are five sound reasons for diversifying faculty within seminaries and Bible schools. I don't think there is a perfect percentage for faculty diversity but aiming for 50 percent as the largest populace of any one ethnicity is a great goal!

Questions for Conversations

TCK:

- Of the noted reasons, which reason would you cite as why you want a minority professor?

- What feelings do you or minority friends have when a school has little to no diversity within leadership and faculty?

Minister/Parent and TCK:

- Have you heard any of these diversity reasons articulated before?
- Of the noted reasons, which one makes the strongest case for you?
- Which reason is the weakest and why?
- How can you prepare/answer naysayers of diversification?
- What key insight did you glean from this section? And how do you plan to integrate the insight into your life/ministry?

WHY IS DIVERSIFYING SO DIFFICULT?

There are numerous reasons why schools have not diversified their faculty and leadership. Five primary issues come to mind. I will list the issue then present a solution to the noted issue.

Ethnicity Is Not on the Mind

I have heard numerous leaders in varying schools say, "why does someone's ethnicity matter." "We should hire the best academic we can, and not care what their ethnicity is." "Purposefully hiring a minority is a type of racism!" Honestly, every time I hear statements such as this, I break down inside for they truly do not understand how much it means to have someone to relate to. Indeed, a faculty member needs to hold a correct degree to gain a job. Once the degree has been vetted, I would encourage thinking about the impact a culturally similar faculty member has upon students. The difference between Christian schools and secular schools is that Christian schools view faculty as ministers who are discipling believers. Thus, why wouldn't a school consider faculty who can better disciple students, through true empathy? If institutions stop at someone's academic credentials, then they are not looking fully at how God has gifted an individual to serve the kingdom! So, to help bring ethnicity to the mind I ask Juan Martinez's question, "What is our vision of God's future? How do we envision the Revelation 7:9–10 worship scene? How does that vision impact how we do church today?"[14]

> Multi-ethnicity is not taught because there is no place for it. There's no one in leadership that truly grasps the Gospel implication. And most of all, we too quickly run to identify in Christ, before fully understand what it is Scripture is saying through their own experience. (Molly L'Hoste)

A Smaller Pool of Candidates

As noted in the Hispanic section of Evangelical Theological Society (ETS) in 2019, most minorities have historically tended toward the Doctor of Ministry program. In the United States, a PhD is the required terminal degree to serve as a faculty member at a grad school. I know of a few exceptions, but they are outliers. All of the minority students that I did master's level work with, who continued into a doctorate program, continued into a DMin not a PhD. As my friends stated, they didn't feel encouraged to enter a PhD program and they felt that they were not adequately prepared for a PhD program. They also thought that DMin prepares one for ministry and PhD prepares one for academics. To supply schools with more PhD minority professors, schools need to prepare, recruit, and encourage students to accomplish a PhD. As stated in the "Hispanic Scholars" section, "schools need to develop a pipeline program." Before outlining ways to build a PhD program, schools need to first articulate to minority students how a PhD can empower one to do ministry or academics, whereas the DMin limits one to ministry. The few PhD minorities that I know have gone into practical fields (i.e., preaching, evangelism, leadership) versus biblical studies and theology. As Matt Akers said, "We need minorities to represent and help the academy in the whole gambit of fields." To accomplish such a program, I encourage having a minority as a minority PhD recruiter for the needed fields. As will be stated later, I suggest having a minority PhD mentor program for PhD students. I suggest empowering PhD minority students when the seminary is asked to speak at conferences. This could mean allowing minority students to go alongside a faculty member to observe and serve as a junior speaker. The hope should be to hire minority faculty to help accomplish all of these, but until a constituency is on campus the PhD students could help serve to represent these minority populaces.

The Cry of the People Makes It Difficult to Leave the Church

Most of my friends who ended up earning a DMin were active in a fulltime pastorate throughout our master's program and their DMin program. In my experience typical minorities in the church do not understand why a pastor would pursue a PhD let alone why they would leave the church to serve as a fulltime professor. I know some schools are hoping to resolve this issue through having "ministerial faculty" positions. However, I have yet to see a school where such a position garners the same respect and impact with students as a typical fulltime faculty member. Therefore, when schools begin the recruiting process, they should help students start thinking differently about the professorate. For me, the professorate is a fulltime ministry. The difference between the church and the academy is that in the academy your people of ministry will be next generation's pastors. This honor needs to be constantly put before the minority recruits and before minority churches when visited, so that respect and honor are given to the minority that chooses to follow this path.

There Is a Huge Pay Difference between the Church and the Academy

Regardless of ethnicity, the reality exists that a church which would hire a doctor as pastor will pay much more than the average school pays a doctor. Seminaries and Bible schools often struggle financially by comparison to large churches. It is doubtful that these institutions will catch up to the senior pastor pay of a large church. Thus, during the recruitment and PhD program students need to be made aware of this financial reality. In every ministry there is some level of suffering. In some ministries the ministry itself is a heavy burden. Within the professorate the burden is often the finances. However, the reality of ministering to future ministers offers the joy of eternal rewards for being kingdom minded.

The Goshen Hesitation

A dear friend of mine, Miguel Echevarria, presented a paper in 2019 at the Evangelical Theological Society, in the Hispanic scholars section. In his paper, he rightly drew parallels between the Israelite initial immigration to Egypt and minority scholars integration within institutions. He termed the parallel "The Goshen problem." The Israelites when they immigrated to Egypt, during the famine and when Joseph was second in command, were welcomed but relegated to Goshen. In parallel, minorities are welcomed into many institutions, but are relegated to a less than desirable location and not purposefully invited into Memphis (the place of leadership). I know of numerous minorities who have been hired by institutions. Though they all hold PhDs in varying fields, all have seemingly been cornered into being strictly minority topic professors. My singular minority professor had a PhD in church history, but rarely taught in the area, because he was moved into being the leader of a race relations dept.

> Confusing racial tokenism with progress provides some denominations and associations with a false sense of progress. To decorate agencies, committees, and staffs with racial minorities, as if they were ornaments on a Christmas tree, so as to give the appearance of progress, is unacceptable. These are tokens, people of color who are invited to strengthen existing systems and further the captivity of the dominant culture. There is a difference between being invited to sit on a committee as a token representative and being asked to lead the

committee, staff, or agency, thus having whites submitting to the authority of people of color.[15]

The numerous minorities that are relegated results in the discouragement of minorities from getting a PhD and pursuing the professorate. Why pursue the hardest doctorate, and struggle to gain a faculty position, only to be relegated to working in minority fields. I advocate for schools to hire minorities to work within their respective fields, not just to be a minority initiative officer.

Questions for Conversations

TCK:

- In your respective culture, is there respect or admiration given to the PhD?
- Why do you think minorities don't pursue PhDs as often as DMins?
- Have you seen the Goshen problem and what impact do you think it has?

Minister/Parent and TCK:

- Which of the five problems is the most commonly stated in your institution?
- Does your school have a pipeline to recruit, train, and empower minority PhDs?
- How has your school historically handled minority professors? How can the school purposefully guard against the Goshen problem?
- What key insight did you glean from this section? And how do you plan to integrate the insight into your life/ministry?

THE TCK IN SEMINARY FACULTY/LEADERSHIP

Like my continual advocation for churches to hire TCKs to move them toward diversity, I continually encourage institutions to do the same! Many of the hesitations from both the school and the candidate are more easily resolved through the nature of TCKs. Here's eight reasons TCKs have the potential to be a great faculty member.[16]

1. They have a cultural diversity that unites differences.
2. They are easy to identify with as leaders.
3. They have the practical skills to communicate with people from various cultures.
4. They have an innate understanding of remote communication and its platforms.

5. They are well-suited to managing change.
6. They are constantly seeking knowledge and understanding.
7. They have enhanced time management skills.
8. They are likely to have grown up with a strong business background.

As a word of testimony, I would like to praise a school I attended, which saw these truths in a candidate. I did predoctoral studies at Mid-America Baptist Theological seminary. When I attended the school, it only had white faculty and white staff. There was a desire to racially diversify for the school sat in Memphis and could speak untold truth via example. If you don't understand the racial complexity of Memphis, you have but to realize that it is the city where Martin Luther King Jr. was killed. Visiting many churches and areas of town I learned of deep-seated mistrust between the races. Though the school was founded as a conservative Baptist school, minority students have attended.

In 2019, MABTS hired Dr. Lee Brand to serve as VP and dean of the seminary. One friend estimated that this makes Dr. Brand the highest ranked minority in SBC life. President Dr. Spradlin told Lee, "I am hiring you to be you! I don't want you to be anyone else." What is interesting though about Dr. Brand is that he is a TCK. He's half white and half black. His academic capability and culturally adaptability bolsters MABTS' sensitivity to both majority and minority faculty and majority and minority students. Brand replied, "I as a mixed person am a bridgebuilder. I can go anywhere you can go theologically, and practically I bring 'street cred.'" In my estimation, Dr. Brands TCK capability makes him the perfect candidate to give such a rank, in such a city, for such a time! I hope and pray that MABTS and my other alma maters will continue to hire minorities in high ranks for the sake of the kingdom. The desire should be for professors, like Brand, who can "walk in and speak to/care for pastors and faculty in varying areas."

HOW AND WHAT SEMINARIES TEACH

When considering how to diversify schools and better equip people to do cross-cultural ministry I have a few suggested changes, beyond faculty diversity.

Biblical Theology

As previously mentioned in chapter 3, Biblical theology helps all believers grasp the grand story of God and their place within the story. This is not only critical for TCKs to grasp their place within the gospel, but this will also aid mono-ethnic believers to grasp how people from other backgrounds fit into the people of God. In 2013 I surveyed decades worth of academic catalogs from the five Southern Baptist seminaries. I was astounded that most of these institutions, decades ago, had three types of theology courses required: historical theology, biblical theology, and systematic theology. Now however, none of the five seminaries require more than systematic theology and few offer the others even as electives. I am by no means advocating for the replacement of systematic theology, but I am advocating for the inclusion of biblical theology. Biblical theology can help students expand their understanding of who the people of God are and as a result develop a more corporate solidarity view of the gospel, rather than only articulating the previously noted personal gospel. When one views the gospel through the lens of corporate solidarity they can't help but be more empathetic of all believers.

Multicultural Ministry/Ecclesiology

I have taken twelve courses on pastoral ministry and ecclesiology. None of these courses even once mentioned minority ministry or ecclesiology. If seminaries desire to be effective at training pastors for ministry and hope that multi-ethnic churches will grow within the United States, then pastors need to be introduced and trained in the ministerial differences.

Brand noted, "I hoped seminary would help me gain the articulation skills of Adrian Rodgers, with the minority cultural application." In order to appropriately cover these different methods of ministry and ecclesiology more textbooks will need to be required and read. If the professor is not personally experienced in these ethnic fields, then outside speakers or other faculty members need to come and speak from firsthand experience. If such a diverse ministry course were developed, how many church debates would be resolved for the pastors will be sympathetic to various backgrounds and articulate when confronted with issues?

History of the Church

Like ministry courses, I have taken numerous church history courses that barely touched the topic of minority history or international third world church history for that matter. Church history 1 covered the early church up to the Reformation. In that time span, I recognize that there is little "third world" recorded history to integrate into the course material. Church history 2, however, covered the Reformation to current day. The only mentioning of Asian, Latin American, or African church history came in the form of European missionaries doing work in these lands. I am grateful for the work of these missionaries, but their legacy did not end when they died, yet the history seems to abruptly end in church history 2. When the latter part of church history 2 covers slavery to civil rights, only a sprinkling of African American church history is presented. In one of my textbooks, this particular church history only covered 15 of the 350 pages of the church history 2 book. Watkins in his chapter discussed similar realities having been the case in seminaries for decades. To counter this imbalance of knowledge Watkins advocates for re-training of current faculty and reorienting of curriculum of the institution.

> This training needs to be in the form of yearlong study initiatives, where faculties are required to read and write from the center of history and theology. The reading and writing initiative must include a complete overhaul of the curriculum-an overhaul that throws off the hegemony of one story by putting it in conversation with the larger, more complete story of two-thirds of the world.[17]

Much like pastoral training courses, to appropriately cover the broader church history more textbooks will be needed and probably more course time too. But imagine the impact this type of global church history would have on all students!

Mentorship

Another suggested course addition comes by way of mentorship.

> Students need mentors and models, not only professors. A praxis model of education will also be strengthened when professors are able to draw from their own ministry and life experience.[18]

Very few schools have mandated mentorship for seminary students. At one of my alma maters the mentors assigned were not carefully thought out. The result was mismatched mentors, especially in the area of ethnic and cultural awareness. I spoke to a Hispanic colleague who attended seminary in the 1980s and he spoke about the woes of not being linguistically understood and not having someone to help guide him through seminary and pastoral preparation. I through my academic career sought out mentorship from scholars and pastors who were known for mentoring. Not only that, but I sought out scholars who were setting an example of what it means to be a minority scholar. Their advice and connections were integral to me building my career to this point. But what if a school doesn't have minority faculty to mentor minority students? I suggest institutions partner minority students with minority scholars and pastors in other places. While mentorship is necessary for all students, especially PhD students who desire to enter academia, I can't overstate how impactful mentorship from minority scholars has been in my life.

Internships

The last suggested course addition would be for all students to serve at least one internship in a church that is ethnically different from theirs. Once again, if we desire to train students to be cross-cultural ministers, then they need cross-cultural experience. While short one-week mission trips can indeed impact someone, a full semester long internship as "the minority" in a different ethnic church will develop empathy within the student for minorities in any context. Not only does empathy develop, but misconceptions can be corrected, and various ministerial and ecclesiological understandings will be gained.

Questions for Conversations

TCK:

- Which field of study do you wish to have a more diverse understanding? (history or ministry)
- If you attended seminary, how could have the addition of biblical theology impacted you?
- When you think of mentors, what do you look for/desire?

Minister/Parent and TCK:

- How does your church/seminary teach theology? Is biblical theology taught?
- What view does your church/institution take to ministry and church history?
- How can your school remedy the mono-cultural education mentioned earlier?
- What do you think will be the hardest aspect to change and why?
- What key insight did you glean from this section? And how do you plan to integrate the insight into your life/ministry?

SUGGESTED READING

"Christian Oneness Today!" by Matthew Akers.
Equally Yoked: A Premarital Counseling Primer for Multiethnic Christian Couples by Matthew Akers.
Crossover Preaching: Intercultural-Improvisational Homiletics in Conversation with Gardner C. Taylor by J. R. Alcántara.
Multicultural Ministry Handbook: Connecting Creatively to a Diverse World by David A. Anderson and Margarita R. Cabellon.

Handbook of Research on Multicultural Education by James A. Banks and Cherry A. McGee Banks.
Aliens in the Promised Land: Why Minority Leadership Is Overlooked in White Christian Churches and Institutions by Anthony Bradley.
Churches, Cultures and Leadership: A Practical Theology of Congregations and Ethnicities Mark Branson and Juan F. Martinez.
"Black + White = Not White: A Minority Bias in Categorizations of Black-White Multiracials" by Jacqueline M. Chen, Kristin Pauker, Sarah E. Gaither, David L. Hamilton, and Jeffrey W. Sherman.
Building a Healthy Multi-Ethnic Church: Mandate, Commitments and Practices of a Diverse Congregation by Mark DeYmaz.
Ethnic Blends: Mixing Diversity into Your Local Church by Mark DeYmaz and Harry Li.
What Are You?: Voices of Mixed-Race Young People by Pearl Fuyo Gaskins.
The 3D Gospel: Ministry in Guilt, Shame, and Fear Cultures by Jayson Georges.
Ministering in Honor-Shame Cultures: Biblical Foundations and Practical Essentials by Jayson Georges and Mark D. Baker.
Intensional: Kingdom Ethnicity in a Divided World by D. A. Horton.
Understanding Biblical Theology: A Comparison of Theory and Practice by Edward Klink and Darian R. Lockett.
A Beginner's Guide to Crossing Cultures: Making Friends in a Multicultural World by Patty Lane.
Ministering Cross-Culturally: A Model for Effective Personal Relationships, 3rd edition, by Sherwood G. Lingenfelter and Marvin K. Mayers.
A Cross-Shaped Gospel: Reconciling Heaven and Earth by Bryan Loritts.
Insider Outsider: My Journey as a Stranger in White Evangelicalism and My Hope for Us All by Bryan Loritts.
A Cross-Shaped Gospel: Reconciling Heaven and Earth by Bryan Loritts.
Right Color, Wrong Culture: The Type of Leader Your Organization Needs to Become Multiethnic by Bryan Loritts.
Pastoral Ministry: How to Shepherd Biblically John F. MacArthur and Master's Seminary Faculty.
"Five Vacancies. Why the SBC Should Hire Its First Minority Entity President" by Dave Miller.
"Multiracial Congregations Have Nearly Doubled, But They Still Lag Behind the Makeup of Neighborhoods" by Media and Public Relations, Baylor University.
On Being a Pastor: Understanding Our Calling and Work by Derek J. Prime, Alistair Begg, and Al Mohler.
"The Social Construction of Race: Biracial Identity and Vulnerability to Stereotypes" by Margaret Shih, Courtney Bonam, Diana Sanchez, and Courtney Peck.
Voices from the Margin: Interpreting the Bible in the Third World by R. S. Sugirtharajah.
Dangerous Calling: Confronting the Unique Challenges of Pastoral Ministry by Paul David Tripp.
Intercultural Theology, Vol. 1: Intercultural Hermeneutics by Henning Wrogemann.

Conclusion
Points of Application

Martin Luther King Jr.'s statement in 1960 of the church divide reigns true today. But as presented in this work, churches are beginning to diversify for numerous reasons: (1) It is a picture of the gospel, (2) it is a picture of heaven on earth, (3) it strengthens the church, (4) it helps the gospel reach to the third generation. While not every church will strive to diversify for each noted reason, the booming population of mixed peoples will necessitate the church to change its ministry methods. With the election of President Obama and the subsequent census change there is a growing awareness of multiethnic-third-cultured peoples in America. Thankfully, research has been recently growing in the psychology and cultural understandings of these multiethnic peoples. The census projects that multi-ethnic people will comprise 20 percent of US population by 2050.

These third cultured people not only necessitate churches considering how they minister, but they also provide churches with uniquely qualified individuals capable of standing in the gap and helping unify the ethnically divided church in America. Through the course of this work, the psychology of third culture syndrome has been presented, and ministerial insight has been provided. Furthermore, third culture ideology has been read back into the context of Timothy in the New Testament. Timothy, like the modern believer, had the unique capability to stand in the gap and help share the gospel in numerous settings, often closed to mono-ethnic believers.

Ministerial changes suggested within this book begin from understanding the context of the TCK believer and culminate with the proposition of empowering TCKs to be pastors for gospel unification sake. In between those two bookends are many ministerial nuances. Thus, the following points of application:

CHAPTER 1 REVIEW POINTS

- Someone of mixed ethnicity can classify as any of the following: third culture kid, biracial, and multiethnic. All of these terms should be utilized when researching mixed peoples.
- TCKs share a number of unique benefits and challenges.
  - Benefits: adaptability, blending in, less prejudice, importance of now, appreciative of authority, observational skills, social skills, linguistic skills, rootlessness, large number of relationships, deep valued relationships
  - Challenges: lack of true cultural balance, defining the difference, more prejudice, delusion of choice, mistrustful of authority, perceived arrogance, restlessness, early maturation, delayed adolescence
- TCKs typically respond to their mixed ethnicity in six noted ways.
- TCKs ask three questions throughout their life: Who am I? Can I Trust? What's wrong with me?
- TCK believers ask three questions throughout their life: Why don't I feel comfortable at my church? Who should I listen to? How does the gospel apply to me?

CHAPTER 2 REVIEW POINTS

- All TCKs have dealt with issues concerning their ethnicity, either in their parent's home or in their own home.
- TCKs are constantly caught between cultures. They will fluctuate throughout their life and sometimes in a given situation.
- TCKs will mature early but have a delayed adolescence due to their third culture upbringing. Thus, the TCK needs more hands-on discipleship than the normal believer.
- TCKs always live in the in-between and struggle with the feeling of restlessness and loneliness their entire life. They subconsciously often feel like a poser due to their mixed nature.
- TCKs struggle to find church to be their home, for it almost never fully represents them.

CHAPTER 3 REVIEW POINTS

- Ministering to a TCK requires a lifetime of intentionally organic discipleship via biblical theology, missional theology, and table theology.
- A church which best ministers to a TCK is one sensitive to diverse ideals of church, leadership.
- A church which retains the TCK member is one with diverse preaching and worship.

CHAPTER 4 REVIEW POINTS

- A church which desires to be multi-ethnic must conquer several fears to hire ministers.
- A TCK pastor can serve as an excellent pastor to help diversify the local church.
- The pulpit is the best place to hire a multi-ethnic pastor! Or I suggest diversifying leadership through equal serving elders, who share the pulpit.
- Selecting a TCK to pastor a multi-ethnic church requires specific examination.
- A TCK pastor requires unique continual encouragements.
- Properly training TCKs to pastor and effect the church divide requires paradigm shifts in seminaries and ministerial schools.
- Diverse faculty is required, because students need mentors and examples more than they need professors.
- Diverse ministerial courses are required so that students may know how to minister across cultural lines.
- Finally, there is a need for continual reminding of the gospel's reconciliation between God and man and believer and believer.

I truly hope this work helps pastors better understand how to minister to mixed peoples just as Paul ministered to Timothy. For me, the mere research and writing of this work has been a means to better understand my mind, struggles, and ways of ministry. While this work is by no means the complete psychological guide, I hope it will provide a foray into the world of TCK studies so that you may help others like me. I hope and pray that you will be able to take the information provided and as a minister, or parent, care for your mixed person in a way that helps them love the gospel and the church. And should the Lord call them into ministry, I pray that they will remember you fondly as I remember my Pauls and undoubtedly Timothy remembered his!

1 Tim. 1:17 τῷ δὲ βασιλεῖ τῶν αἰώνων, ἀφθάρτῳ, ἀοράτῳ, μόνῳ θεῷ, τιμὴ καὶ δόξα εἰς τοὺς αἰῶνας τῶν αἰώνων · ἀμήν.

Notes

INTRODUCTION

1. Lawrence Spivak, *Martin Luther King Jr. on Meet the Press*, April 17, 1960, http://okra.stanford.edu/transcription/document_images/Vol05Scans/17Apr1960_InterviewonMeetthePress.pdf.

2. "Multiracial Congregations Have Nearly Doubled, But They Still Lag Behind the Makeup of Neighborhoods," *Media and Public Relations | Baylor University*, June 20, 2018, https://www.baylor.edu/mediacommunications/news.php?action=storystory=199850.

3. "Multiracial Congregations Have Nearly Doubled."

4. Gretchen Livingston and Anna Brown, "Trends and Patterns in Intermarriage," *Pew Research Center's Social Demographic Trends Project*, May 18, 2017, https://www.pewsocialtrends.org/2017/05/18/1-trends-and-patterns-in-intermarriage/.

5. Kim Parker, Juliana Horowitz, Rich Morin, and Mark Lopez, "Multiracial in America: Proud, Diverse and Growing in Numbers," *Pew Research Center's Social Demographic Trends Project*, June 2015, https://www.pewsocialtrends.org/2015/06/11/multiracial-in-america/.

6. Livingston and Brown, "Trends and Patterns in Intermarriage."

7. Parker et al., "Multiracial in America."

8. David C. Pollock and Ruth E. Van Reken, *Third Culture Kids: Growing Up among Worlds*, Revised (Boston, MA: Nicholas Brealey, 2009), 13–14.

9. Jennifer Latson, "The Biracial Advantage," *Psychology Today*, n.d., https://www.psychologytoday.com/articles/201905/the-biracial-advantage.

10. Bryan Loritts, *Right Color, Wrong Culture: The Type of Leader Your Organization Needs to Become Multiethnic* (Chicago, IL: Moody Publishers, 2014), 201.

11. "Five Vacancies. Why the SBC Should Hire Its First Minority Entity President," *SBC Voices*, October 11, 2018, https://sbcvoices.com/five-vacancies-why-the-sbc-should-hire-its-first-minority-entity-president/.

12. Jemar Tisby, "The Joyful Pursuit of Multi-Ethnic Churches," *The Gospel Coalition*, n.d., https://www.thegospelcoalition.org/article/the-joyful-pursuit-of-multi-ethnic-churches/.

13. Mark DeYmaz and Harry Li, *Ethnic Blends: Mixing Diversity into Your Local Church* (Grand Rapids, MI: Zondervan, 2010), 37.

14. DeYmaz and Li, *Ethnic Blends*, 127.

15. Matt Carter and Darrin Patrick, *For the City: Proclaiming and Living Out the Gospel* (Grand Rapids, MI: Zondervan, 2011).

16. Matt Akers, "Christian Oneness Today!," *Salmerica*, n.d.

17. Sandra L. Richter, *The Epic of Eden: A Christian Entry into the Old Testament* (Downers Grove, IL: IVP Academic, 2008), 104.

CHAPTER 1

1. Kristin Pauker and Nalini Ambady, "Multiracial Faces: How Categorization Affects Memory at the Boundaries of Race," *The Journal of Social Issues* 65, no. 1 (2009), http://search.ebscohost.com/login.aspx?direct=truedb=cmedmAN=24311822site=ehost-live.

2. Sarah E. Gaither, "'Mixed' Results: Multiracial Research and Identity Explorations," *Current Directions in Psychological Science* 24 (2015): 114–19.

3. John Useem, Ruth Useem, and John Donoghue, "Men in the Middle of the Third Culture," *The International Executive* 6 (1964): 17–18.

4. Pollock and Van Reken, *Third Culture Kids*, 15–17.

5. M. Langford, "Global Nomads, Third Culture Kids, and International Schools," in *International Education: Principles and Practice* (London: Psychology Press, 1998), 28–43.

6. Trevor Grimshaw and Coreen Sears, "'Where Am I from?' 'Where Do I Belong?' The Negotiation and Maintenance of Identity by International School Students," *Journal of Research in International Education* 7, no. 3 (2008): 259–78; Mary Hayden, *Introduction to International Education: International Schools and Their Communities* (London: SAGE, 2006).

7. A. D. Lee, *Teaching and Learning around the Cycle: An Experiential Model for Intercultural Training for Cross-Cultural Kids* (Diss., Biola University, n.d.); Pollock and Van Reken, *Third Culture Kids*.

8. L. R. Frederick, *Balancing the Four Major Influences on Transcultural Students through an Educational Environment* (Diss., University of Georgia, 1996).

9. Pollock and Van Reken, *Third Culture Kids*.

10. M. J. Klemens, *Psychological Well-Being, Ethnic Identity, and Sociocultural Adaptation in College-Aged Missionary Kids* (Diss., Seattle Pacific University, 2008); T. N. Schulz, *A Study to Determine the Basic Needs of MK's upon Re-Entry to the United States and to Define and Describe a Re-Entry Program Designed to Meet the Needs (Missionary Children, Third Culture, International)* (Diss., University of Nebraska, 1985); J. S. Sotherden, *The Reentry of "Third Culture Kids" into*

the United States (Diss., University of Houston, 1992); S. J. Thurston-Gonzalez, *A Qualitative Investigation of the College Choice Experiences and Reentry Expectations of U.S. American Third Culture Kids* (Diss., Loyola University, 2009); K. Wrobbel, *The University-Level Academic Success of Missionary Kids Educated in Second-Language Host Country National Schools* (Diss., University of Minnesota, n.d.).

11. Allyn D. Lyttle, Gina G. Barker, and Terri Lynn Cornwell, "Adept through Adaptation: Third Culture Individuals' Interpersonal Sensitivity," *International Journal of Intercultural Relations* 35, no. 5 (2011): 686–94; A. M. Moore, *Confused or Multicultural: A Phenomenological Analysis of the Self-Perception of Third Culture Kids with Regard to Their Cultural Identity* (MA thesis, Liberty University, 2011); B. Schaetti, *Global Nomad Identity: Hypothesizing a Developmental Model* (Diss., Union Institute, n.d.).

12. H. Fail, *An Examination of the Life Histories of a Group of Former International School Students* (Diss., University of Bath, n.d.).

13. Ulrika Ernvik, *Third Culture Kids: A Gift to Care For* (Familjegladje, 2019).

14. David C. Pollock, *The T.C.K. Profile: Seminar with David C. Pollock* (Upland, IN: Taylor Video Production for Interaction, Inc., 1988).

15. Pollock and Van Reken, *Third Culture Kids*, 31–32.

16. Barack Obama, *Dreams from My Father* (New York, NY: Three Rivers, 2004).

17. Sarah E. Gaither, Leigh S. Wilton, and Danielle M. Young, "Perceiving a Presidency in Black (and White): Four Years Later," *Analyses of Social Issues and Public Policy (ASAP)* 14 (2014): 7–21.

18. Gaither, "'Mixed' Results"; Sarah E. Gaither, Jessica D. Remedios, Diana T. Sanchez, and Samuel R. Sommers, "Thinking Outside the Box: Multiple Identity Mind-Sets Affect Creative Problem Solving," *Social Psychological and Personality Science* 6 (2015): 596–603.

19. Ernvik, *Third Culture Kids*, 43–45.

20. Chi-Ying Cheng and Fiona Lee, "Multiracial Identity Integration: Perceptions of Conflict and Distance among Multiracial Individuals," *Journal of Social Issues* 65 (2009): 51–68.

21. Ernvik, *Third Culture Kids*, 49–50.

22. Courtney M. Bonam and Margaret Shih, "Exploring Multiracial Individuals' Comfort with Intimate Interracial Relationships," *Journal of Social Issues* 65 (2009): 87–103.

23. Ernvik, *Third Culture Kids*, 115.

24. Ernvik, *Third Culture Kids*, 115.

25. Ernvik, *Third Culture Kids*, 115.

26. Ernvik, *Third Culture Kids*, 117.

27. Loritts, *Right Color, Wrong Culture*, 201.

28. Ernvik, *Third Culture Kids*, 49.

29. Ernvik, *Third Culture Kids*, 51.

30. Parker et al., "Multiracial in America."

CHAPTER 2

1. Parker et al., "Multiracial in America."
2. H. R. Markus, C. M. Steele, and D. M. Steele, "Color Blindness as a Barrier to Inclusion," in *Engaging Cultural Differences: The Multicultural Challenge in Liberal Democracies* (New York, NY: Russell Sage Foundation, 2002), 453–72.
3. Phillip Atiba Goff, M. C. Jackson, A. H. Nichols, and B. A. L. Di Leone, "Anything but Race: Avoiding Racial Discourse to Avoid Hurting You or Me," *Psychology* 4 (2013): 335–39.
4. Parker et al., "Multiracial in America."
5. Joseph G. Ponterotto and C. Kerwin, "Biracial Identity Development: Theory and Research," in *Handbook of Multicultural Counseling* (Thousand Oaks, CA: SAGE Publications, 1995), 199–217.
6. Cheng and Lee, "Multiracial Identity Integration," 51–68.
7. Gaither, "'Mixed' Results," 114–19.
8. Parker et al., "Multiracial in America."
9. Parker et al., "Multiracial in America."
10. Susan Black, "Bilingual Education: Melting Pot or Salad Bowl," *Education Digest* 60, no. 7 (1995): 53; L. S. Greenberg, "Unity in Diversity: Salad Bowl, Not Melting Pot," *Contemporary Psychology* 40, no. 7 (1995): 644–45; Lisa M. Leslie, J. E. Bono, Y. S. Kim, and G. R. Beaver, "On Melting Pots and Salad Bowls: A Meta-Analysis of the Effects of Identity-Blind and Identity-Conscious Diversity Ideologies," *Journal of Applied Psychology* 105, no. 5 (2020): 453–71; Bruce Thornton, "Melting Pots and Salad Bowls," Text, *Hoover Institution*, n.d., https://www.hoover.org/research/melting-pots-and-salad-bowls.
11. Bonam and Shih, "Exploring Multiracial Individuals'," 87–103.
12. Latson, "The Biracial Advantage."
13. Parker et al., "Multiracial in America."
14. Pollock and Van Reken, *Third Culture Kids*, 211–28.
15. Pollock and Van Reken, *Third Culture Kids*, 153–58.
16. Pollock and Van Reken, *Third Culture Kids*, 158–59.
17. Parker et al., "Multiracial in America."
18. Pollock and Van Reken, *Third Culture Kids*, 140.
19. Helen Fail, "Why Business Needs Our Third Culture Kids," *Telegraph*, June 20, 2002, https://www.telegraph.co.uk/expat/4188135/Why-business-needs-our-third-culture-kids.html.
20. Latson, "The Biracial Advantage."
21. Parker et al., "Multiracial in America."
22. Parker et al., "Multiracial in America."
23. Kevin R. Binning, Miguel M. Unzueta, Yuen J. Huo, and Ludwin E. Molina, "The Interpretation of Multiracial Status and Its Relation to Social Engagement and Psychological Well-Being," *Journal of Social Issues* 65 (2009): 35–49.
24. Pollock and Van Reken, *Third Culture Kids*, 162.
25. Kevin D. Dougherty and Michael O. Emerson, "The Changing Complexion of American Congregations," *Journal for the Scientific Study of Religion* 57, no. 1 (2018): 24–38.

CHAPTER 3

1. Francis Chan, Mark Beuving, and David Platt, *Multiply: Disciples Making Disciples* (Colorado Springs, CO: David C. Cook, 2012); Robby Gallaty, Chris Swain, and Robert E. Coleman, *Replicate: How to Create a Culture of Disciple-Making Right Where You Are* (Chicago, IL: Moody Publishers, 2020); Bobby Harrington, Alex Absalom, and Thom Rainer, *Discipleship That Fits: The Five Kinds of Relationships God Uses to Help Us Grow* (Grand Rapids, MI: Zondervan, 2016).
2. Ernvik, *Third Culture Kids*, 39.
3. Ernvik, *Third Culture Kids*, 39.
4. Ernvik, *Third Culture Kids*, 39.
5. Ernvik, *Third Culture Kids*, 295.
6. Ernvik, *Third Culture Kids*, 141.
7. Graeme Goldsworthy, *The Goldsworthy Trilogy* (Eugene, OR: Wipf and Stock, 2014), 45–46.
8. "Five Vacancies."
9. Anthony Bradley, "General Introduction: My Story," in *Aliens in the Promised Land* (Philipsburg, NJ: P R Publishing, 2013), 23.

CHAPTER 4

1. Dougherty and Emerson, "The Changing Complexion," 24–38.
2. Juan Martinez, "Serving Alongside Latinos in A Multiethnic, Transnational, Rapidly Changing World," in *Aliens in the Promised Land* (Philipsburg, NJ: P R Publishing, 2013), 70.
3. Bradley, "General Introduction," 24.
4. DeYmaz and Li, *Ethnic Blends*, 46.
5. Sarah E. Gaither, Negin R. Toosi, Laura G. Babbitt, and Samuel R. Sommers, "Exposure to Biracial Faces Reduces Colorblindness," *Personality and Social Psychology Bulletin* 45 (2019): 54–66.
6. Bonam and Shih, "Exploring Multiracial Individuals," 87–103.
7. David A. Anderson and Margarita R. Cabellon, *Multicultural Ministry Handbook: Connecting Creatively to a Diverse World* (Downers Grove, IL: IVP, 2010), 17, http://site.ebrary.com/id/10833480.
8. Anderson and Cabellon, *Multicultural Ministry Handbook*, 17.
9. Soong-Chan Rah, *Next Evangelicalism: Freeing the Church from Western Cultural Captivity* (Downers Grove, IL: IVP, 2014), http://qut.eblib.com.au/patron/FullRecord.aspx?p=2033945.
10. Amos Yong, "Race and Racialization in a Post-Racist Evangelicalism: A View from Asian America," in *Aliens in the Promised Land* (Philipsburg, NJ: P R Publishing, 2013), 56.
11. Sarah E. Gaither, Eva E. Chen, Kathleen H. Corriveau, Paul L. Harris, Nalini Ambady, and Samuel R. Sommers, "Monoracial and Biracial Children: Effects of Racial Identity Saliency on Social Learning and Social Preferences," *Child Development* 85 (2014): 2299–2316.

12. "Multiracial Congregations Have Nearly Doubled."

13. Anthony Bradley, "Afterword," in *Aliens in the Promised Land* (Philipsburg, NJ: P R Publishing, 2013), 151.

14. Martinez, "Serving Alongside Latinos," 70.

15. Bradley, "General Introduction," 23–24.

16. Humphries, "8 Reasons Third Culture Kids Have the Potential to Be Great Leaders," *Lifehack*, June 3, 2015, https://www.lifehack.org/articles/productivity/8-reasons-third-culture-kids-have-the-potential-great-leaders.html.

17. Ralph Watkins, "A Black Church Perspective on Minorities in Evangelicalism," in *Aliens in the Promised Land* (Philipsburg, NJ: P R Publishing, 2013), 127.

18. Martinez, "Serving Alongside Latinos," 67.

Bibliography

Akers, Matthew R. "Christian Oneness Today!" *Salmerica*, n.d.
———. *Equally Yoked: A Premarital Counseling Primer for Multiethnic Christian Couples*. Eugene, OR: Wipf & Stock, 2016.
Albuja, Analia F., Sarah E. Gaither, Diana T. Sanchez, Brenda Straka, and Rebecca Cipollina. "Psychophysiological Stress Responses to Bicultural and Biracial Identity Denial." *Journal of Social Issues* 75, no. 4 (2019): 1165–1191.
Alcántara, Jared E. *Crossover Preaching: Intercultural-Improvisational Homiletics in Conversation with Gardner C. Taylor*. Downers Grove, IL: IVP Academic, 2015.
Anderson, David A., and Margarita R. Cabellon. *Multicultural Ministry Handbook: Connecting Creatively to a Diverse World*. Downers Grove, IL: IVP, 2010.
Axt, Jordan R., Charles R. Ebersole, and Brian A. Nosek. "The Rules of Implicit Evaluation by Race, Religion, and Age." *Psychological Science* 25 (2014): 1804–1815.
Babbitt, Laura G., Sarah E. Gaither, Negin R. Toosi, and Samuel R. Sommers. "The Role of Gender in Racial Meta-Stereotypes and Stereotypes." *Social Cognition* 36, no. 5 (2018): 589–601.
Banks, James A., and Cherry A. McGee Banks. *Handbook of Research on Multicultural Education*. San Francisco, CA: Jossey-Bass, Inc., 2004.
Binning, Kevin R., Miguel M. Unzueta, Yuen J. Huo, and Ludwin E. Molina. "The Interpretation of Multiracial Status and Its Relation to Social Engagement and Psychological Well-Being." *Journal of Social Issues* 65 (2009): 35–49.
Bonam, Courtney M., and Margaret Shih. "Exploring Multiracial Individuals' Comfort with Intimate Interracial Relationships." *The Journal of Social Issues* 65 (2009): 87–103.
Bonhoeffer, Dietrich. *Life Together*. Translated by Daniel W. Bloesch. Minneapolis, MN: Fortress Press, 2015.
———. *The Cost of Discipleship*. New York, NY: Touchstone, 2018.

Bradley, Anthony. *Aliens in the Promised Land: Why Minority Leadership Is Overlooked in White Christian Churches and Institutions*. Philipsburg, NJ: P&R Publishing, 2013.

Branson, Mark, and Juan F. Martinez. *Churches, Cultures and Leadership: A Practical Theology of Congregations and Ethnicities*. Downers Grove, IL: IVP Academic, 2011.

Brawner, Jeff. *How to Share Christ with Your Friends of Another Faith*. Garland, TX: Hannibal Books, 2012.

Brunsma, David L., ed. *Mixed Messages: Multiracial Identities in the "Color-Blind" Era*. Boulder, CO: Lynne Rienner Publishers, 2005.

Carter, Matt, and Darrin Patrick. *For the City: Proclaiming and Living Out the Gospel*. Grand Rapids, MI: Zondervan, 2011.

Chan, Francis, Mark Beuving, and David Platt. *Multiply: Disciples Making Disciples*. Colorado Springs, CO: David C. Cook, 2012.

Chen, Jacqueline M., Kristin Pauker, Sarah E. Gaither, David L. Hamilton, and Jeffrey W. Sherman. "Black + White = Not White: A Minority Bias in Categorizations of Black-White Multiracials." *Journal of Experimental Social Psychology* 78 (2018): 43–54.

Cheng, Chi-Ying, and Fiona Lee. "Multiracial Identity Integration: Perceptions of Conflict and Distance among Multiracial Individuals." *Journal of Social Issues* 65 (2009): 51–68.

DeYmaz, Mark. *Building a Healthy Multi-Ethnic Church: Mandate, Commitments and Practices of a Diverse Congregation*. San Francisco, CA: Jossey-Bass, 2013.

———. *Multiethnic Conversations: An Eight-Week Journey toward Unity in Your Church*. Middletown, CT: Wesleyan Publishing House, 2016.

———. *Re:MIX: Transitioning Your Church to Living Color*, 2016. http://public.e bookcentral.proquest.com/choice/publicfullrecord.aspx?p=4355450.

DeYmaz, Mark, and Harry Li. *Ethnic Blends: Mixing Diversity into Your Local Church*. Grand Rapids, MI: Zondervan, 2010.

Dougherty, Kevin D., and Michael O. Emerson. "The Changing Complexion of American Congregations." *Journal for the Scientific Study of Religion* 57, no. 1 (2018): 24–38.

Dukes, Kristin Nicole, and Sarah E. Gaither. "Black Racial Stereotypes and Victim Blaming: Implications for Media Coverage and Criminal Proceedings in Cases of Police Violence against Racial and Ethnic Minorities." *Journal of Social Issues* 73, no. 4 (2017): 789–807.

Easley, Kendell H. *Holman Illustrated Guide to Biblical History: With Photos from the Archives of the Biblical Illustrator*. Edition Unstated edition. Nashville, TN: Holman Reference, 2003.

Ernvik, Ulrika. *Third Culture Kids: A Gift to Care For*. Familjegladje, 2019.

Fail, Helen. *An Examination of the Life Histories of a Group of Former International School Students*. Diss., University of Bath, 2002.

———. "Why Business Needs Our Third Culture Kids." *Telegraph*, June 20, 2002. https://www.telegraph.co.uk/expat/4188135/Why-business-needs-our-third-cult ure-kids.html.

Frederick, L. R. *Balancing the Four Major Influences on Transcultural Students through an Educational Environment*. Diss., University of Georgia, 1996.

Gaither, Sarah E. "'Mixed' Results: Multiracial Research and Identity Explorations." *Current Directions in Psychological Science* 24 (2015): 114–119.

———. "The Multiplicity of Belonging: Pushing Identity Research beyond Binary Thinking." *Self & Identity* 17, no. 4 (2018): 443–454.

Gaither, Sarah E., Laura G. Babbitt, and Samuel R. Sommers. "Resolving Racial Ambiguity in Social Interactions." *Journal of Experimental Social Psychology* 76 (2018): 259–269.

Gaither, Sarah E., Eva E. Chen, Kathleen H. Corriveau, Paul L. Harris, Nalini Ambady, and Samuel R. Sommers. "Monoracial and Biracial Children: Effects of Racial Identity Saliency on Social Learning and Social Preferences." *Child Development* 85, no. 6 (2014): 2299–2316.

Gaither, Sarah E., Jacqueline M. Chen, Kristin Pauker, and Samuel R. Sommers. "At Face Value: Psychological Outcomes Differ for Real vs Computer-Generated Multiracial Faces." *The Journal of Social Psychology* 159 (2019): 592–610.

Gaither, Sarah E., Kristin Pauker, Michael L. Slepian, and Samuel R. Sommers. "Social Belonging Motivates Categorization of Racially Ambiguous Faces." *Social Cognition* 34 (2016): 97–118.

Gaither, Sarah E., Jessica D. Remedios, Diana T. Sanchez, and Samuel R. Sommers. "Thinking Outside the Box: Multiple Identity Mind-Sets Affect Creative Problem Solving." *Social Psychological and Personality Science* 6 (2015): 596–603.

Gaither, Sarah E., Samuel R. Sommers, and Nalini Ambady. "When the Half Affects the Whole: Priming Identity for Biracial Individuals in Social Interactions." *Journal of Experimental Social Psychology* 49, no. 3 (2013): 368–371.

Gaither, Sarah E., Negin R. Toosi, Laura G. Babbitt, and Samuel R. Sommers. "Exposure to Biracial Faces Reduces Colorblindness." *Personality and Social Psychology Bulletin* 45 (2019): 54–66.

Gallaty, Robby. *Growing Up: How to Be a Disciple Who Makes Disciples*. Nashville, TN: B & H, 2013.

Gallaty, Robby, Chris Swain, and Robert E. Coleman. *Replicate: How to Create a Culture of Disciple-Making Right Where You Are*. Chicago, IL: Moody Publishers, 2020.

Gaskins, Pearl Fuyo. *What Are You?: Voices of Mixed-Race Young People*. New York, NY: Henry Holt, 1999. https://archive.org/details/whatareyouvoices00gask.

Georges, Jayson. *The 3D Gospel: Ministry in Guilt, Shame, and Fear Cultures*. Amerika: Time Press, 2014.

Georges, Jayson, and Mark D. Baker. *Ministering in Honor-Shame Cultures: Biblical Foundations and Practical Essentials*. Downers Grove, IL: IVP Academic, 2016.

Goldsworthy, Graeme. *According to Plan: The Unfolding Revelation of God in the Bible*. Softcover edition. Downers Grove, IL: IVP Academic, 2002.

———. *The Goldsworthy Trilogy*. Eugene, OR: Wipf and Stock, 2014.

Grimshaw, Trevor, and Coreen Sears. "'Where Am I from?' 'Where Do I Belong?' The Negotiation and Maintenance of Identity by International School Students." *Journal of Research in International Education* 7, no. 3 (2008): 259–278.

Harrington, Bobby, Alex Absalom, and Thom Rainer. *Discipleship That Fits: The Five Kinds of Relationships God Uses to Help Us Grow*. Grand Rapids, MI: Zondervan, 2016.

Hayden, Mary. *Introduction to International Education: International Schools and Their Communities*. London: SAGE, 2006.

Hayden, Mary, and Jeff Thompson. *International Education: Principles and Practice*. London: Psychology Press, 1998.

Hitlin, Steven, J. Scott Brown, and Glen H. Elder Jr. "Racial Self-Categorization in Adolescence: Multiracial Development and Social Pathways." *Child Development* 77 (2006): 1298–1308.

Holton, Eve M. *Stages of Biracial Identity Formation: Positive Findings by a Multiracial Doctor*. Scotts Valley, CA: CreateSpace Independent, 2011.

Horton, D. A. *Intensional: Kingdom Ethnicity in a Divided World*. Colorado Springs, CO: NavPress, 2019.

Howell, Jennifer L., Sarah E. Gaither, and Kate A. Ratliff. "Caught in the Middle: Defensive Responses to IAT Feedback among Whites, Blacks, and Biracial Black/Whites." *Social Psychological and Personality Science* 6, no. 4 (2015): 373–381.

Humphries, Lewis. "8 Reasons Third Culture Kids Have the Potential to Be Great Leaders." *Lifehack*, June 3, 2015. https://www.lifehack.org/articles/productivity/8-reasons-third-culture-kids-have-the-potential-great-leaders.html.

Jackson, Bailey. *New Perspectives on Racial Identity Development: Integrating Emerging Frameworks*. 2nd edition. Edited by Charmaine L. Wijeyesinghe. New York, NY: NYU Press, 2012.

Jones, Edward A., and Theological Research Exchange Network. *Preaching to a Multi-Ethnic Audience to Build Unity*, 2013.

Jones, Rachel. *Finding Home: Third Culture Kids in the World*. Seattle, WA: KDP Print US, 2018.

Kerwin, Christine, Joseph G. Ponterotto, Barbara L. Jackson, and Abigail Harris. "Racial Identity in Biracial Children: A Qualitative Investigation." *Journal of Counseling Psychology* 40 (1993): 221–231.

Kim, Eunjoo Mary, and Mark R. Francis CSV. *Christian Preaching and Worship in Multicultural Contexts: A Practical Theological Approach*. Collegeville, MN: Pueblo Books, 2017.

Klemens, M. J. *Psychological Well-Being, Ethnic Identity, and Sociocultural Adaptation in College-Aged Missionary Kids*. Diss., Seattle Pacific University, 2008.

Klink, Edward, and Darian R. Lockett. *Understanding Biblical Theology: A Comparison of Theory and Practice*. Grand Rapids, MI: Zondervan, 2012.

Kristen, A. Renn. "Patterns of Situational Identity Among Biracial and Multiracial College Students." *Review of Higher Education* 23, no. 4 (2000): 399–420.

Lane, Patty. *A Beginner's Guide to Crossing Cultures: Making Friends in a Multicultural World*. Downers Grove, IL: IVP Books, 2002.

Langford, M. "Global Nomads, Third Culture Kids, and International Schools." Pages 28–43 in *International Education: Principles and Practice*. London: Psychology Press, 1998.

Latson, Jennifer. "The Biracial Advantage." *Psychology Today*, 2019. https://www.psychologytoday.com/articles/201905/the-biracial-advantage.

Lee, A. D. *Teaching and Learning around the Cycle: An Experiential Model for Intercultural Training for Cross-Cultural Kids*. Diss., Biola University, 2008.

Lingenfelter, Sherwood G., and Marvin K. Mayers. *Ministering Cross-Culturally: A Model for Effective Personal Relationships*. 3rd edition. Grand Rapids, MI: Baker Academic, 2016.

Linton, Dale B. "International Christian Schoolteachers' Traits, Characteristics, and Qualities Valued by Third Culture Kids." *JRCE* 24, no. 3 (2015): 190–211.

Livingston, Gretchen, and Anna Brown. "Trends and Patterns in Intermarriage." *Pew Research Center's Social & Demographic Trends Project*, May 18, 2017. https://www.pewsocialtrends.org/2017/05/18/1-trends-and-patterns-in-intermarriage/.

Loritts, Bryan C. *Right Color, Wrong Culture: The Type of Leader Your Organization Needs to Become Multiethnic*. Chicago, IL: Moody Publishers, 2014.

———. *A Cross-Shaped Gospel: Reconciling Heaven and Earth*. Chicago, IL: Moody Publishers, 2011.

———. *Insider Outsider: My Journey as a Stranger in White Evangelicalism and My Hope for Us All*, 2018. http://rbdigital.rbdigital.com.

Loyd, Aerika Brittian, and Sarah E. Gaither. "Racial/Ethnic Socialization for White Youth: What We Know and Future Directions." *Journal of Applied Developmental Psychology* 59 (2018): 54–64.

Lyttle, Allyn D., Gina G. Barker, and Terri Lynn Cornwell. "Adept through Adaptation: Third Culture Individuals' Interpersonal Sensitivity." *International Journal of Intercultural Relations* 35, no. 5 (2011): 686–694.

MacArthur, John F., and Master's Seminary Faculty. *Pastoral Ministry: How to Shepherd Biblically*. Nashville, TN: Thomas Nelson, 2017.

Markus, H. R., C. M. Steele, and D. M. Steele. "Color Blindness as a Barrier to Inclusion." Pages 453–472 in *Engaging Cultural Differences: The Multicultural Challenge in Liberal Democracies*. New York, NY: Russell Sage Foundation, 2002.

Marti, Gerardo. *Worship across the Racial Divide: Religious Music and the Multiracial Congregation*. Oxford: Oxford University Press, 2018.

Marzouk, Safwat. *Intercultural Church: A Biblical Vision for an Age of Migration*. Minneapolis, MN: Fortress Press, 2019.

McCaig, Norma. "Growing Up with a World View: Nomad Children Develop Multicultural Skills." *Foreign Service Journal* 9 (1994): 32–41.

Miller, Dave. "Five Vacancies. Why the SBC Should Hire Its First Minority Entity President." *SBC Voices*, October 11, 2018. https://sbcvoices.com/five-vacancies-why-the-sbc-should-hire-its-first-minority-entity-president/.

Mills, Melinda. *The Borders of Race: Patrolling "Multiracial" Identities*. Boulder, CO: Lynne Rienner Publishers, 2020.

Moore, A. M. *Confused or Multicultural: A Phenomenological Analysis of the Self-Perception of Third Culture Kids with Regard to Their Cultural Identity*. MA thesis, Liberty University, 2011.

Morrison, Jhonetta Wade. "Developing Identity Formation and Self-Concept in Preschool-Aged Biracial Children." *Early Child Development and Care* 111 (1995): 141–152.

Muller, Roland. *Honor and Shame: Unlocking the Door*. Philadelphia, PA: Xlibris, 2001.

"Multiracial Congregations Have Nearly Doubled, But They Still Lag Behind the Makeup of Neighborhoods." *Media and Public Relations, Baylor University*, June 20, 2018. https://www.baylor.edu/mediacommunications/news.php?action=story&story=199850.

Nathan, Peter E., Verónica Benet-Martínez, and Ying-Yi Hong. *The Oxford Handbook of Multicultural Identity*. Oxford: Oxford University Press, 2014.

Nayani, Farzana, Dr. Velina Hasu Houston, and Dr. Paul Spickard. *Raising Multiracial Children: Tools for Nurturing Identity in a Racialized World*. Berkeley, CA: North Atlantic Books, 2020.

Newby, Stephen Michael. *Worship Outside the Music Box: Theology of Music & Worship and Multi-Ethnic Ministry*. Enumclaw, WA: Redemption Press, 2015.

Obama, Barack. *Dreams from My Father*. New York, NY: Three Rivers, 2004.

Parker, Kim, Juliana Horowitz, Rich Morin, and Mark Lopez. "Multiracial in America: Proud, Diverse and Growing in Numbers." *Pew Research Center's Social & Demographic Trends Project*, June 2015. https://www.pewsocialtrends.org/2015/06/11/multiracial-in-america/.

Pauker, Kristin, and Nalini Ambady. "Multiracial Faces: How Categorization Affects Memory at the Boundaries of Race." *The Journal of Social Issues* 65, no. 1 (2009): 69–86.

Pauker, Kristin, Nalini Ambady, and Jonathan B. Freeman. "The Power of Identity to Motivate Face Memory in Biracial Individuals." *Social Cognition* 31, no. 6 (2013): 780–791.

Pauker, Kristin, Colleen Carpinella, Chanel Meyers, Danielle M. Young, and Diana T. Sanchez. "The Role of Diversity Exposure in Whites' Reduction in Race Essentialism over Time." *Social Psychological and Personality Science* 9, no. 8 (2018): 944–952.

Pauker, Kristin, Chanel Meyers, Diana T. Sanchez, Sarah E. Gaither, and Danielle M. Young. "A Review of Multiracial Malleability: Identity, Categorization, and Shifting Racial Attitudes." *Social and Personality Psychology Compass* 12, no. 6 (2018): 1–15.

———. "A Review of Multiracial Malleability: Identity, Categorization, and Shifting Racial Attitudes." *Social & Personality Psychology Compass* 12, no. 6 (2018): 1–1.

Piper, John. *Let the Nations Be Glad!: The Supremacy Of God In Missions*. 3rd edition. Grand Rapids, MI: Baker Academic, 2010.

Pollock, David C. *The T.C.K. Profile: Seminar with David C. Pollock*. Upland, IN: Taylor Video Production for Interaction, Inc., 1988.

Pollock, David C., and Ruth E. Van Reken. *Third Culture Kids: Growing Up among Worlds*. Revised. Boston, MA: Nicholas Brealey, 2009.

Ponterotto, Joseph G. *Handbook of Multicultural Counseling*. Thousand Oaks, CA: SAGE Publications, 2010.

Ponterotto, Joseph G., and C. Kerwin. "Biracial Identity Development: Theory and Research." Pages 199–217 in *Handbook of Multicultural Counseling*. Thousand Oaks, CA: SAGE Publications, 1995.

Prime, Derek J., Alistair Begg, and Al Mohler. *On Being a Pastor: Understanding Our Calling and Work*. New edition. Chicago, IL: Moody Publishers, 2013.

Renn, Kristen. "Patterns of Situational Identity Among Biracial and Multiracial College Students." *Review of Higher Education* 23, no. 4 (2000): 399–420.

Richter, Sandra L. *The Epic of Eden: A Christian Entry into the Old Testament*. Downers Grove, IL: IVP Academic, 2008.

Roccas, Sonia, and Marilynn B. Brewer. "Social Identity Complexity." *Personality & Social Psychology Review (Lawrence Erlbaum Associates)* 6, no. 2 (2002): 88–106.

Rockquemore, Kerry Ann. "Negotiating the Color Line: The Gendered Process of Racial Identity Construction among Black/White Biracial Women." *Gender & Society African American Women: Gender Relations, Work, and the Political Economy in the Twenty-First Century* 16, no. 4 (2002): 485–503.

Rockquemore, Kerry Ann, and David L. Brunsma. "Negotiating Racial Identity: Biracial Women and Interactional Validation." *Women & Therapy* 27, no. 1/2 (2004): 85.

———. "Socially Embedded Identities: Theories, Typologies, and Processes of Racial Identity among Black/White Biracials." *Sociological Quarterly* 43, no. 3 (2002): 335.

Rockquemore, Kerry Ann, David L. Brunsma, and Daniel J. Delgado. "Racing to Theory or Retheorizing Race? Understanding the Struggle to Build a Multiracial Identity Theory." *Journal of Social Issues* 65, no. 1 (2009): 13–34.

Sanchez, Diana T., and Courtney M. Bonam. "To Disclose or Not to Disclose Biracial Identity: The Effect of Biracial Disclosure on Perceiver Evaluations and Target Responses." *Journal of Social Issues* 65, no. 1 (2009): 129–149.

Schaetti, B. *Global Nomad Identity: Hypothesizing a Developmental Model*. Diss., Union Institute, 2000.

Schulz, T. N. *A Study to Determine the Basic Needs of MK's upon Re-Entry to the United States and to Define and Describe a Re-Entry Program Designed to Meet the Needs (Missionary Children, Third Culture, International)*. Diss., University of Nebraska, 1985.

Sebring, Deborah L. "Considerations in Counseling Interracial Children." *Journal of Non-White Concerns in Personnel & Guidance* 13, no. 1 (1985): 3–9.

Shih, Margaret, Courtney Bonam, Diana Sanchez, and Courtney Peck. "The Social Construction of Race: Biracial Identity and Vulnerability to Stereotypes." *Cultural Diversity & Ethnic Minority Psychology* 13, no. 2 (2007): 125–133.

Shih, Margaret, and Diana T. Sanchez. "Perspectives and Research on the Positive and Negative Implications of Having Multiple Racial Identities." *Psychological Bulletin* 131, no. 4 (2005): 569–591.

Sotherden, J. S. *The Reentry of "Third Culture Kids" into the United States*. Diss., University of Houston, 1992.

Spencer, Rainier. *Challenging Multiracial Identity*. Boulder, CO: Lynne Rienner Publishers, 2006.

Spivak, Lawrence. *Martin Luther King Jr. on Meet the Press*, April 17, 1960. http://okra.stanford.edu/transcription/document_images/Vol05Scans/17Apr1960_InterviewonMeetthePress.pdf.

Sugirtharajah, R. S. *Voices from the Margin: Interpreting the Bible in the Third World*. Maryknoll, NY: Orbis Books, 2016.

Terry, John Mark, ed. *Missiology: An Introduction*. Revised edition. Grand Rapids, MI: B & H Academic, 2015.

Thurston-Gonzalez, S. J. *A Qualitative Investigation of the College Choice Experiences and Reentry Expectations of U.S. American Third Culture Kids*. Diss., Loyola University, 2009.

Tisby, Jemar. "The Joyful Pursuit of Multi-Ethnic Churches." *The Gospel Coalition*, n.d. https://www.thegospelcoalition.org/article/the-joyful-pursuit-of-multi-ethnic-churches/.

Townsend, Sarah, Stephanie A. Fryberg, Clara L. Wilkins, and Hazel Rose Markus. "Being Mixed: Who Claims a Biracial Identity?" *Cultural Diversity & Ethnic Minority Psychology* 18, no. 1 (2012): 91–96.

Townsend, Sarah S. M., Hazel R. Markus, and Hilary B. Bergsieker. "My Choice, Your Categories: The Denial of Multiracial Identities." *Journal of Social Issues* 65, no. 1 (2009): 185–204.

Tripp, Paul David. *Dangerous Calling: Confronting the Unique Challenges of Pastoral Ministry*. Wheaton, IL: Crossway, 2012.

Twine, France Winddanc. "Brown Skinned White Girls: Class, Culture and the Construction of White Identity in Suburban …." *Gender, Place & Culture: A Journal of Feminist Geography* 3, no. 2 (1996): 205.

Useem, John, Ruth Useem, and John Donoghue. "Men in the Middle of the Third Culture." *The International Executive* 6 (1964): 17–18.

Wilkins, Clara L., Cheryl R. Kaiser, and Heather Rieck. "Detecting Racial Identification: The Role of Phenotypic Prototypicality." *Journal of Experimental Social Psychology* 46, no. 6 (2010): 1029–1034.

Wright, Marguerite. *I'm Chocolate, You're Vanilla: Raising Healthy Black and Biracial Children in a Race-Conscious World*. San Francisco, CA: Jossey-Bass, 2000.

Wrobbel, K. *The University-Level Academic Success of Missionary Kids Educated in Second-Language Host Country National Schools*. Diss., University of Minnesota, 2005.

Wrogemann, Henning. *Intercultural Theology, Vol. 1: Intercultural Hermeneutics*. Translated by Karl E. Böhmer. Downers Grove, IL: IVP Academic, 2016.

———. *Intercultural Theology, Vol. 2: Theologies of Mission*. Downers Grove, IL: IVP Academic, 2018.

Index

abilities/capabilities, 14, 21, 23, 34, 71, 97
adaptability, 20, 41, 42
adolescence, 40–41
anchors/disciplers, 55–59, 66–68, 80, 113
anxiety, 30, 45
arrogance, 18, 42
aversion, 38

belonging, 22, 56, 78, 107
benefits, 15, 18, 19, 41
biblical theology, 60–64, 119, 120, 122
blending in, 18, 41, 43, 126

comfort, 44, 46–48, 62, 64, 66, 74
commonality/common, 3–5, 8, 19, 22, 25–26, 33–34, 47–48, 54, 58, 66, 73–74, 85, 103, 108, 118
communication, 18, 40
community, 22, 31–32, 35, 47, 49, 54, 76, 77
confusion, 44, 61

decision making, 73–74
discipleship, 26, 53–68, 107, 110, 113
diversify, 6, 27, 38, 46, 48, 78, 80, 81, 84, 90, 99, 100, 104, 112, 115, 119

early maturity, 18, 37, 40, 41
emotions/feelings, 34–35, 43–44
encouragement, 17, 36, 58, 66–71, 88
ethnicity, 1, 5, 7, 41, 46, 49, 73–75, 79, 90, 115

family: parents, 30–36; personal, 37–39

gospel, 5–12, 27, 48–50, 53, 57, 62, 64–67, 89, 104, 114–15, 119–20

leadership, 4, 42, 46–47, 49, 68, 72, 74, 80, 84–85, 96, 98, 100–102, 112, 114–18
linguistic diversity, 81
loneliness, 44, 80, 108

marriage, 1, 3, 10, 27, 31–32, 35–39, 70
mentorship, 110, 122
missional theology, 60, 63–65
mono-ethnic, 5, 10, 18, 21, 22, 27, 34, 37, 39–42, 48, 75, 78–79, 90, 99–101, 110, 120

New Testament, 6, 9, 63, 69, 76, 82, 100–102, 106

Old Testament, 55

peers, 19–21, 40, 106
politics, 36, 84, 86–88, 96, 98
preaching, 53, 59, 75, 77, 79, 83–84, 86, 87, 89, 97, 102, 106
preference(s), 33, 37

question(s), 21, 30, 40, 43, 53, 60–61, 96, 98, 105–9, 111, 126
Questions for Conversations, 10, 17, 26–27, 39, 42, 49, 59, 61, 63, 65, 72, 75, 78, 80, 82, 85, 89, 91, 100, 110, 114, 118, 122

racial identity, 42, 98
racism, 29, 96, 115
reconcile, 104
representation, 59, 62, 79–81

season, 45, 46
seminary, 95, 110–14, 118–23
sensitivity, 4, 25, 38, 53, 75, 83, 86, 101, 113, 119

Southern Baptist/SBC, 1, 3, 95–99, 119–20, 123
Star Trek, 3, 4, 22–25
story, 3, 33, 56–57, 61–63, 104, 106, 119
subculture, 16

table theology, 60, 61, 66–68
third culture history/definitions, 14
Third Culture Kids: description, 14; experience, 16, 23, 30, 31, 34, 38, 42, 55–57, 61, 121–22; friends, 21, 22, 30, 32, 35, 38, 40–48, 62, 106, 108; needs, 17, 36, 55–56, 59, 90

view(s)(ed), 31–42, 44, 47, 50, 55, 72–78, 81, 84, 86, 88, 98, 101, 106, 113, 115, 120

worship, 59, 67, 70, 74, 76–78, 81, 83–84, 86, 88, 90–93, 98, 113, 115, 126

About the Author

Mario Manuel Catalino Melendez is the Auguie Henry Chair of Old Testament and Biblical Studies at Oklahoma Baptist University. He is Filipino and Cajun French and grew up around the deaf community. He has served as a minority ministry strategist, Hispanic youth intern, and Bible study writer for a refugee church. He also lectures on the topic of multiethnic ministry. He is a member of the Hispanic Theological Educators section of the Evangelical Bible Society and the guidance committee for the Deaf Bible Society, which seeks to increase deaf ministers' access to formal theological education.

www.ingramcontent.com/pod-product-compliance
Lightning Source LLC
Chambersburg PA
CBHW051542230426
43669CB00015B/2698